STAR TREK MANIA!

It's time to explore new ~~~ ~~~ swers. Use your impulse ~~~ following STAR TREK st~~~

- What was the name of the leader responsible for the theft of Spock's brain?
- The *Enterprise* visited what planet in "And the Children Shall Lead?
- Fatigue and depression were the two major effects of the virus in "Immunity Syndrome". True or False?
- Yeoman Rand became the obsessive desire of young Charlie in what episode?
- Which Star Trek character wore a beard in "Mirror, Mirror"?
- Captain Kirk's cabin was on what deck of the *Enterprise* in the TV series?
- "Revenge is a dish that is best served cold" is whose proverb?
- Kirk communicates with the cloud creature with a universal _____.
- The sight of the Medusa without a protective visor can cause what?
- What was the real name of Spock's favorite "pet" as a child?

For answers to these and more than 1,000 others, keep on reading—at warp speed! You'll find that this is the logical way to fill your memory banks with TRIVIA MANIA!

TRIVIA MANIA: TV GREATS

TRIVIA MANIA: I LOVE LUCY   (1730, $2.50)

TRIVIA MANIA: THE HONEYMOONERS   (1731, $2.50)

TRIVIA MANIA: STAR TREK   (1732, $2.50)

TRIVIA MANIA: THE DICK VAN
DYKE SHOW   (1733, $2.50)

TRIVIA MANIA: MARY TYLER MOORE   (1734, $2.50)

TRIVIA MANIA: THE ODD COUPLE   (1735, $2.50)

Available wherever paperbacks are sold, or order direct from the Publisher. Send cover price plus 50¢ per copy for mailing and handling to Zebra Books, Dept. 1732, 475 Park Avenue South, New York, N.Y. 10016. DO NOT SEND CASH.

STAR TREK

TRIVIA Mania

BY XAVIER EINSTEIN

ZEBRA BOOKS
KENSINGTON PUBLISHING CORP.

A special thanks to Carol I. Henson, without whose help this book could not have been written. And to Barbara Johnson and Jane Singer.

ZEBRA BOOKS

are published by

Kensington Publishing Corp.
475 Park Avenue South
New York, N.Y. 10016

First printing: September 1985

Printed in the United States of America

TRIVIA MANIA:
Star Trek

1) The *Enterprise*'s original mission was for how many years?

2) Mr. Sulu was played by what actor?

3) What actor portrayed Capt. Christopher Pike?

4) When Lieutenant Savik accuses Spock of lying in *Star Trek II: The Wrath of Khan*, Spock's reply is "I _____."

5) The leader in "Way To Eden" is a carrier of what disease?

6) The aging process in "The Deadly Years", restored what regional accent to Dr. McCoy?

7) According to Sarek in *Star Trek III*, Mr. Spock entrusted Admiral Kirk with his _____.

8) What invention does the "parallel Kirk" use in "Mirror, Mirror" to do away with his enemies?

... *Answers*

1. Five years

2. George Takei

3. Jeffery Hunter

4. Exaggerated

5. Sythococus Nouae

6. Southern

7. Katra

8. Tantalus Field

9) What caused the damage to the probe in "The Changeling"?

10) What actor portrayed Decker in "The Doomsday Machine"?

11) In the ritual combat of "Amok Time", Spock must fight whom to the death?

12) What is the name of the alien Captain Kirk was forced to fight in "Arena"?

13) No one was supposed to visit what planet in "The Menagerie"?

14) In *Star Trek: The Motion Picture*, V'ger sent a probe in the form of whom?

15) What episode gives the only view of the Shuttle-bay Observation Deck?

16) What was the name of the giant android in "What Are Little Girls Made Of"?

17) At first, Cochran is pleased by the Cloud Creature's feelings for him in "Metamorphosis". True or false?

18) Who receives the first Vulcan Nerve pinch ever executed on Earth, in "City On The Edge of Forever"?

. . . Answers

9. A meteor

10. William Windom

11. Kirk

12. The Gorn

13. Talos IV

14. Lt. Ilia

15. "Conscience Of The King"

16. Ruk

17. False

18. A policeman

19) At what speed does the *Enterprise* have to travel back to the planet in "Paradise Syndrome"?

20) Which of the following was turned into the planet Vulcan for the shooting of *Star Trek II*?
    a. The Los Angeles Public Library
    b. Universal Studio's back lot
    c. Occidental College
    d. None of the above

21) Kirk allows Seven to detonate the rocket over Earth in "Assignment: Earth" at the last possible moment. True or false?

22) What is the name of Gill's subversive aide in "Patterns of Force"?

23) What is the name of the leader of the Kelvans in "By Any Other Name"?
    a. Kojac
    b. Rojan
    c. Landru
    d. Flint

24) The creature in "Immunity Syndrome" is a one-celled life form about to —
    a. surrender
    b. explode
    c. divide
    d. scream

. . . *Answers*

19. Sublight

20. c

21. True

22. Melakon

23. b

24. c

25) Who must Kirk fight when he makes a wager with the Providers in "The Gamesters of Triskelion"?

26) What form of measurement do the Klingons in *Star Trek III* utilize to determine distance in space?
   a. Kilagrams
   b. Keltigrams
   c. Kelicams
   d. none of the above

27) What STAR TREK actress portrayed Margaret Anderson in FATHER KNOWS BEST?

28) What has Merik's name been changed to in "Bread and Circuses"?

29) Complete this line of dialog from "The Trouble With Tribbles". "Who put the Tribbles in the _____"?

30) Identical twins were cast in "I, Mudd" and used to make the "Alice" android series. True or false?

31) Black Arban is the material that composed the hull of "The Doomsday Machine". True or false?

32) Mara was the Science Officer on whose ship?
   a. Kirk's
   b. Kang's
   c. Sarek's

33) How many Klingons were in the Klingon search party sent to Genesis in *Star Trek III*?

. . . Answers

25. Shahna

26. c

27. Jane Wyatt

28. First Citizen Merikus

29. Quadrotriticale

30. True

31. False

32. b

33. Three

34) What planet does the *Enterprise* visit in "This Side of Paradise"?

35) What weapon did the Federation Ambassador finally use to help Kirk destroy the computers in "Taste of Armageddon"?

36) What actor portrayed Sandoval in "This Side of Paradise"?

37) What is being mined in "Devil in the Dark"?

38) Odona dies before Kirk can find an antidote in "Mark of Gideon". True or false?

39) Which of Sulu's shoulders was injured by the alien's touch in "That Which Survives"?

40) What actor portrayed Kang in "Day of the Dove"?

41) Mr. Chekov suffers an injury to his left hand, in *Star Trek: The Motion Picture*. True or false?

42) Name the two missing researchers whom the *Enterprise* crew searches for in "The Empath".
   a. Linke and Ozaba
   b. Flint and Mothman
   c. Locke and Ozgood

43) After viewing tapes of their parents' graves in "The Children Shall Lead", the children watch the entity turn ugly. True or false?

. . . Answers

34. Omicron Ceti III

35. Sonic Disruptor

36. Frank Overton

37. Pergium

38. False

39. Left

40. Michael Ansara

41. False

42. a

43. True

44) In "Tomorrow is Yesterday", Captain Christopher must return to Earth in his own time frame because of his yet-to-be born _____.

45) Paramount Pictures, at one time, considered making *Star Trek III* in 3-D. True or false?

46) What was Mudd's full name in "Mudd's Women"?

47) What is the name of the secret project to be tested in *Star Trek II: The Wrath of Khan*?

48) George Takei and his family were sent to a Japanese-American relocation camp during World War II. True or false?

49) Jeffrey Hunter starred in STAR TREK episode #1, "The Cage". True or false?

50) In what century does the action take place in *Star Trek II: The Wrath of Khan*?

51) Captain Kirk and Mr. Scott travel to the *Enterprise* via a travel pod in *Star Trek: The Motion Picture*. True or false?

52) What character lures Kirk to Camus II because of her hatred for him in "Turnabout Intruder"?

53) Dr. Sevrin is cured of his disease once he reaches his Eden in "Way to Eden". True or false?

. . . Answers

44. Son

45. True

46. Harcourt Fenton Mudd

47. Genesis

48. True

49. True

50. 23rd

51. True

52. Janice Lester

53. False

QUESTIONS

54) Captain Kirk returns to his youthful self while on the bridge in "The Deadly Years". True or false?

55) What actress portrayed the captain's woman in "Mirror, Mirror"?

56) What was the name of the alien probe encountered by Nomad in "The Changeling"?

57) What is the crew counterpart of a Bird of Prey in *Star Trek III*?
    a. 10
    b. 12
    c. 15
    d. 20

58) What composer's music is predominant in "The Doomsday Machine"?

59) Who gives Kirk the injection that stops the fighting in "Amok Time"?

60) On what planet did the battle between Kirk and the Gorn take place in "Arena"?

61) Who was ordered court-martialed in "The Menagerie"?

62) What was Karidian's daughter's first name in "Conscience of the King"?

. . . *Answers*

54. False

55. Barbara Luna

56. TanRu

57. b

58. Sol Kaplan

59. Dr. McCoy

60. Cestus 3

61. Spock

62. Lenore

63) What actor portrayed Ruk in "What Are Little Girls Made Of"?

64) In "Friday's Child", Eleen's response to Dr. Mc-Coy's "The child is mine", is "The child is _____".

65) Commander Decker utilizes _____ to destroy the asteroid in the wormhole in *Star Trek: The Motion Picture*.
    a. a photon torpedo
    b. a heavy phaser blast
    c. a telepathic directive
    d. none of the above

66) The Vulcan Principle IDIC stands for what?

67) What two aliens are responsible for the trick or treating in "Cat's Paw"?
    a. Koridian and Sarnak
    b. Korob and Sylvia
    c. Sarek and Spock
    d. Kornak and Sylvia

68) Rodent uses what to destroy himself in "City on the Edge of Forever"?

69) Who does Kirk marry in "The Paradise Syndrome"?

70) What actor portrayed Gary Seven in "Assignment: Earth"?

. . . *Answers*

63. Ted Cassidy

64. Yours

65. b

66. Infinite Diversity in Infinite Combinations

67. b

68. McCoy's phaser

69. Miramanee

70. Robert Lansing

QUESTIONS

71) What is the name of the nearby planet being persecuted by Melakon in "Patterns of Force"?

72) How many years would it take the Kelvans in "By Any Other Name" to get back to their own galaxy?

73) The only guest star in "Immunity Syndrome" is the one-celled creature. True or false?

74) Uhura is left in the hands of what character in "The Gamesters of Triskelon"?

75) What actor portrayed Thelev in "Journey to Babel"?

76) What is the name of the Empire's proconsul in "Bread and Circuses"?

77) What was Barris's full title in "Trouble With Tribbles"?

78) What two actresses portrayed the Alice android series in "I, Mudd"?
   a. Rhae and Alyce Andrece
   b. Alice and Roberta Andrews
   c. Jane and Susan Wyatt

. . . Answers

71. Zeon

72. 300

73. True

74. Lars, The Drill Thrall

75. William O'Connell

76. Claudius Marcus

77. Federation Undersecretary of Agricultural Affairs

78. a

QUESTIONS

79) What does 97.835 megatons refer to?
    a. the weight of the Starship *Enterprise*
    b. the explosion created by short circuiting a star-ship's engines
    c. General Order Seven
    d. the doomsday machine

80) An antique helmet played an important part in Scotty's leisure drinking. Why?
    a. He hid his prize bottle of Scotch there
    b. He wore it while drinking
    c. He drank ceremoniously from it

81) The colonists in "This Side of Paradise" had been exposed to what deadly rays?

82) What actor portrayed Anan 7 in "Taste of Armageddon"?

83) What alcoholic beverage was Dr. McCoy enjoying in "This Side of Paradise"?

84) What real-life tragedy befell William Shatner during filming of "The Devil in the Dark"?

85) Dr. McCoy finally locates Captain Kirk and brings him back to the *Enterprise* in "Mark of Gideon". True or false?

86) What actress portrayed Losira in "That Which Survives"?

. . . Answers

79. b

80. a

81. Berthold

82. David Opatoshu

83. Mint Julep

84. Father's death

85. False

86. Lee Meriweather

87) What is the only STAR TREK television episode to show a female Klingon?

88) What two aliens kidnap Kirk, Spock and McCoy in "The Empath"?
   a. Ruk and Roger
   b. Lal and Thann
   c. Thrall and Losira

89) The Gorgan tells the children in "The Children Shall Lead" that he is "the friendly _____".

90) Name Captain Christopher's unborn son in "Tomorrow Is Yesterday".

91) In what episode did Dr. McCoy first utter the now famous line "He's dead, Jim".?

92) What was the date on the bottle McCoy gave Kirk for his birthday in *Star Trek II: The Wrath of Khan*?

93) What STAR TREK actor has appeared with both Cary Grant and John Wayne in major motion pictures?

94) Gene Roddenberry is considered the creator/producer of STAR TREK. True or false?

95) Who directed *Star Trek II: The Wrath of Khan*?

96) Captain Kirk's mind is trapped in what character's body in "Turnabout Intruder"?

. . . *Answers*

87. "Day Of The Dove"

88. b

89. Angel

90. Sean Jeffrey Christopher

91. "Enemy Within"

92. 2283

93. George Takei

94. True

95. Nicholas Meyer

96. Dr. Janice Lester

QUESTIONS

97) What deadly fever breaks out aboard the *Enterprise* in "Requiem for Methuselah"?

98) What did McCoy say he had removed from sick bay in anticipation of Mr. Spock's taking the antidote in "Deady Years"?

99) What is the character name of the captain's woman's counterpart in "Mirror, Mirror"?

100) *Nomad's* original mission was to seek out alien life in the universe. True or false?

101) What will be Captain Christopher's son's rank as discovered in "Tomorrow is Yesterday"?

102) In "The Doomsday Machine", when Kirk reminds Decker that the third planet no longer exists, Decker responds, "Don't you think _____ _____ _____!"

103) The injection given Kirk in "Amok Time" simulates what?

104) Name the aliens who place Kirk and the alien captain at odds in "Arena".

105) What Starbase Commodore in "The Menagerie" helps Captain Kirk overtake the *Enterprise*?

106) Who is discovered as the real murderer of the *Tarsus IV* survivors in "Conscience of the King"?

. . . *Answers*

97. Rigellian Fever

98. All breakables

99. Lt. Marlena Moreau

100. True

101. Captain

102. I know that

103. Death

104. Metrons

105. Mendez

106. Lenore

QUESTIONS

107) STAR TREK's Ted Cassidy portrayed what character in the TV series THE ADDAMS FAMILY?

108) What appears to be holding the *Enterprise* motionless in the opening of "Who Mourns for Adonais"?

109) What actor portrayed Cochran in "Metamorphosis"?

110) Which of the two aliens helps Kirk and company escape in "Cat's Paw"?

111) What actress portrayed Edith Keeler in "City on the Edge of Forever"?

112) What is the title of Kirk's wife in "The Paradise Syndrome"?

113) What actress portrayed Roberta Lincoln in "Assignment: Earth"?

114) Who was Kirk's former history teacher in "Patterns of Force"?

115) Into what geometric shape were many of the *Enterprise* crew members turned into in "By Any Other Name"?

116) Complete Spock's line of dialogue in "Immunity Syndrome". "Tell McCoy he should have _____ _____ _____".

. . . Answers

107. Lurch

108. A green hand

109. Glenn Corbett

110. Korob

111. Joan Collins

112. Priestess

113. Teri Garr

114. John Gill

115. Tetrahedon

116. Wished me luck

QUESTIONS

117) What character is assigned to Mr. Chekov in "Gamesters of Triskelon"?

118) The *Enterprise* journeys to what planet in "A Private Little War"?

119) Kirk mistakes Septimus's people to be _____ worshipers in "Bread and Circuses".

120) What was the name of the Federation representative in charge of the grain shipment in "Trouble With Tribbles"?

121) What episode was Samuel Matlovsky's only composing assignment in STAR TREK?

122) Copper is the basis for Spock's blood. True or false?

123) What was the character name of the colony leader in "This Side of Paradise"?

124) What actress portrayed Mea in "A Taste of Armageddon"?

125) What actor played Mr. Leslie in "This side of Paradise"?

126) What actor portrayed Vanderberg in "Devil in the Dark"?

. . . Answers

117. Tamoon

118. Neural

119. Sun

120. Nilz Barris

121. "I, Mudd"

122. True

123. Elias Sandoval

124. Barbara Babcock

125. Eddie Paskey

126. Ken Lynch

127) What was the title of the first major motion picture to feature the STAR TREK television series characters?

128) Working to prevent an explosion in "That Which Survives", Scotty referred to Spock as what type of time piece?

129) What planet sent a distress call to the *Enterprise* in "Plato's Stepchildren"?

130) What is the name of the young woman Kirk and crew encounter in "The Empath"?

131) What actor portrayed Gorgan in "And The Children Shall Lead"?

132) In "Tomorrow Is Yesterday", it is discovered that Sean Christopher would lead an important expedition into space. True or false?

133) In the episode "Enemy Within", what Vulcan "weapon" did viewers see in action for the first time?

134) What was the name of the starship Khan commandeered in *Star Trek II*?

135) Helmsman Sulu was originally Physicist Sulu. True or false?

136) STAR TREK was the first TV series Gene Roddenberry ever produced. True or false?

. . . Answers

127. *Star Trek: The Motion Picture*

128. Coo-coo clock

129. Platonius

130. Gem

131. Melvin Belli

132. True

133. Nerve Pinch

134. *Reliant*

135. True

136. False

QUESTIONS

137) The *Enterprise* bridge seen in the opening of *Star Trek II*, is really a simulator. True or false?

138) McCoy and Scotty are charged with mutiny and given what sentence in "Turnabout Intruder"?

139) What is the fever's antidote in "Requiem For Methuselah"?

140) What is the name of the android who takes over the *Enterprise* controls in "I, Mudd"?

141) What planet is visited by the *Enterprise* in "The Deadly Years"?

142) Tanru's original purpose was to seek sterilized soil samples in "The Changeling". True or false?

143) Scotty's line ". . . thirty seconds later . . . poooff!" in "Doomsday Machine", is delivered minus a Scottish accent. True or false?

144) What actress portrayed T'Pau in "Amok Time"?

145) The voice of the Metrons in "Arena" is the same voice heard in the introduction to the series, THE OUTER LIMITS. True or false?

146) A visit to the planet Spock was heading for in "The Menagerie", would demand what Federation penalty?

. . . Answers

137. True

138. Death Penalty

139. Ryetalyn

140. Norman

141. Gamma Hydra IV

142. True

143. True

144. Celia Lousky

145. True

146. Death

147) In "Conscience of the King", Karidan never permitted himself to be seen off stage. True or false?

148) What is the name of the progressive penal colony in "Dagger of the Mind"?

149) What character "holds" the *Enterprise* in "Who Mourns for Adonais"?

150) What STAR TREK actor portrayed Linc Chase in the TV series ROUTE SIXTY-SIX?

151) The first mission to Saturn will be led by
    a. Captain Kirk's unborn son
    b. Captain Christopher's unborn son
    c. Khan's unborn son

152) *Nomad* was the creation of inventor
    a. Kirk
    b. Daystrom
    c. Roykirk
    d. Walley

153) The actor who portrayed Mr. Spinelli in "Space Seed" portrayed what character in "The Changeling"?

154) With what neighboring planet were the Eminians at war in "Taste of Armageddon"?

. . . Answers

147. True

148. Tantalus Five

149. Apollo

150. Glenn Corbett

151. b

152. c

153. Mr. Singh

154. Vendikar

155) In *Star Trek: The Motion Picture* beings of Lt. Ilia's race must take an oath of _____ before serving aboard a Federation vessel.

   a. honor
   b. celibacy
   c. obedience
   d. No special oath is necessary

156) The huge doors of the council room in "Errand of Mercy", open by themselves during the entire episode. True or false?

157) Name the creature in "Devil in the Dark".

158) Kirk is transported down to an exact duplicate of what ship in "Mark of Gideon"?

159) What is the name of the geologist who is killed in "That Which Survives"?

160) McCoy's fatal disease is cured in "The World Is Hollow And I Have Touched The Sky". True or false?

161) What does Spock forget to use when viewing the Medusan in "Is There No Truth In Beauty"?

162) How had the scientists died in "The Children Shall Lead"?

163) After Charlie has difficulty with an *Enterprise* yeoman, Dr. McCoy suggests Captain Kirk talk to him about what?

. . . *Answers*

155. b

156. True

157. Horta

158. *Enterprise*

159. Lt. D'Amato

160. True

161. Visor

162. Suicide

163. Birds and bees (mating)

164) What character remained on board the alien's ship as a sort of "cultural exchange student" in "The Corbomite Maneuver"?

165) In *Star Trek II*, what is *Reliant*'s serial number?

166) James Doohan's first STAR TREK appearance as Montgomery Scott was in which episode?
    a. "The Cage"
    b. "Where No Man Has Gone Before"
    c. "The Ultimate Computer"
    d. "The Corbomite Maneuver"

167) What STAR TREK actor portrayed Jesus in the 1961 MGM classic, *King of Kings*?

168) In *Star Trek II*, what is *Reliant*'s prefix number/code?

169) Mr. Spock leaves the *Enterprise* in *Star Trek: The Motion Picture* to investigate V'ger's interior, alone, at Kirk's request. True or false?

170) What is the name of the woman found in the ice age in "All Our Yesterdays"?

171) What is the name of the stolen spaceship discovered in "Way to Eden"?

172) What actress portrayed Lt. Arlene Galway in "Deadly Years"?

. . . Answers

164. Mr. Bailey

165. NCC 1864

166. b

167. Jeffrey Hunter

168. 16309

169. False

170. Zarabeth

171. *Aurora*

172. Beverly Washburn

173) What malfunctions in "Mirror, Mirror", creating a problem for the *Enterprise* crew?

174) The computer/probe in "The Changeling", mistakes Kirk for its _____.

175) Who rigs the self-destruct switch on the *Constellation* in "The Doomsday Machine"?

176) "Koon-ut-kal-if-fee" is the ceremony, "marriage or challenge" in "Amok Time". True or false?

177) What actor portrayed Trelane in "Squire of Gothos"?

178) In "Court Martial", Lieutenant Shaw wears the only female dress uniform seen in the TV series. True or false?

179) What was the suspected real name of Karidian in "Conscience of the King"?

180) Although Kirk orders phasers to be used in "Balance of Terror", the optical effect shown is that of photon torpedoes. True or false?

181) In *Star Trek: The Motion Picture*, V'ger is _____ hours away from Earth when Kirk briefs the crew in the rec room.

    a. 48.3   c. 72.1
    b. 61.9   d. 53.4

. . . *Answers*

173. Transporter

174. Creator

175. Kirk

176. True

177. William Campbell

178. True

179. Kodos

180. True

181. d

QUESTIONS

182) Mr. Spock does not go through the "terrible ordeal" of holding a human baby in "Friday's Child". True or false?

183) The cloud creature gives up its status on the planet because of what feeling for Cochrane in "Metamorphosis"?

184) On what planet does the action in "Cat's Paw" take place?

185) The script for "City On The Edge of Forever" won the Writer's Guild of America Award for most outstanding dramatic episodic teleplay for 1967-68. True or false?

186) Who volunteers her cabin for Elaan in "Elaan of Troyius"?

187) What is the name of the character who materializes aboard the *Enterprise* claiming to be from Earth in "Assignment: Earth"?

188) What is the name of the historian sent by the Federation to the planet in "Patterns of Force"?

189) What is the slang term used for car in "Piece of the Action"?

190) The life form in "Immunity Syndrome" is discovered to be a _____.

. . . Answers

182. False

183. Love

184. Pyris VII

185. True

186. Lieutenant Uhura

187. Gary Seven

188. John Gill

189. Flivver

190. Virus

191) The games staged in "Gamesters of Triskelon" are for whose amusement?

192) Spock's favorite pet as a child is commonly referred to by Terrans as a _____ _____.

193) What planet does the *Enterprise* crew visit in "Bread and Circuses"?

194) Who wrote "Trouble With Tribbles"?

195) In *Star Trek III*, Fal Tor Pan is described by T'Lar as
    a. refusion
    b. diffusion
    c. fission
    d. fusion

196) What is Mudd's wife's first name in "I, Mudd"?

197) Quatlos were the form of currency used in which episode?
    a. "The Cloud Minders"
    b. "The Cage"
    c. "The Gamesters of Triskelion"
    d. "The Ultimate Computer"

. . . Answers

191. The Providers

192. Teddy bear

193. 892-IV

194. David Gerrold

195. a

196. Stella

197. c

198) The mind would be blank if you allowed the machine in this episode to be used. What episode was it?

    a. "Operation: Annihilate"
    b. "The City On The Edge of Forever"
    c. "Dagger of the Mind"
    d. "The Cage"

199) Isis was assistant to Gary Seven in what episode?

200) Admiral Kirk meets with Admiral _____ before taking command of the *Enterprise* in *Star Trek: The Motion Picture*.

201) What actor portrayed Mr. Spinelli in "Space Seed"?

202) The war in "Taste of Armageddon" was fought with _____.

203) Complete Spock's line to Liela in "This Side of Paradise". "I can _____ _____".

204) What were the creatures' eggs made of in "Devil in the Dark"?

205) What is the name of the beautiful woman Kirk finds alone in "Mark of Gideon"?

. . . *Answers*

198. c

199. "Assignment: Earth"

200. Nogura

201. Blaisdell Makee

202. Computers

203. Love you

204. Silicon

205. Odona

206) *Star Trek III* ends with the following printed message:
    a. "The Human Adventure Continues"
    b. "And the Adventure Continues"
    c. "The Human Adventure is Just Beginning"
    d. None of the above

207) Which well known yeoman lived in room 3C46?
    a. Syrena Gorde
    b. Dorothy Fontane
    c. Janice Rand
    d. Stacey Walley

208) How many tricorders did the landing party have in "That Which Survives"?

209) What actress portrayed Natira in "The World is Hollow And I Have Touched The Sky"?

210) Vadia Potenza portrays Mr. Spock at age nine in *Star Trek III*. True or false?

211) Why can Jones view the Medusa without protecting her eyes in "Is There No Truth In Beauty"?

212) The *Enterprise* visited what planet in "And the Children Shall Lead"?

213) Kirk must return the *Enterprise* and crew to their own time without changing history in "Tomorrow is Yesterday". True or false?

. . . Answers

206. b

207. c

208. Three

209. Katherine Woodville

210. False

211. She's blind

212. Triacus

213. True

214) How many women accompanied Mudd on board the *Enterprise* in "Mudd's Women"?

215) What private transmit station does Kirk suggest to Uhura in "Operation: Annihilate"?
    a. GSK 783-Subspace Frequency 3
    b. GSK 783-Subspace Frequency 9
    c. GGS 783
    d. None of the above

216) What Canadian STAR TREK actor was a decorated pilot in World War II?

217) Jeffrey Hunter wore a "time travel belt" in what movie in 1966, opposite France Nuyen?

218) Mr. Scott's portion of the destruct sequence seen in *Star Trek III*, is:
    a. Destruct Sequence Two, Code 11A2B3
    b. Destruct Sequence Three, Code 1A2B
    c. Destruct Sequence Two, Code 1A2B
    d. Destruct Sequence Two, Code 1A2B3

219) Who, in *Star Trek II*, is discovered to have been the only Starfleet cadet ever to beat "the no-win scenario"?

220) The ice age woman in "All Our Yesterdays", follows McCoy and Spock back to the library. True or false?

221) What planet are the young people seeking in "Way To Eden"?

. . . Answers

214. Three

215. a

216. Doohan

217. *Dimension Five*

218. c

219. James T. Kirk

220. False

221. Eden

222) Who portrayed Laura Johnson in "Deadly Years"?

223) What four crew members experienced a parallel universe in "Mirror, Mirror"?
    a. Spock, Uhura, Scotty, Sulu
    b. Kirk, McCoy, Scotty, Uhura
    c. Uhura, Kirk, Chekov, Sulu
    d. None of the above

224) What was the name of the computer's real scientist/creator in "The Changeling"?

225) Kirk plays back what to show Decker wasn't always an insane commander in "Doomsday Machine"?
    a. the library tape
    b. the starship log
    c. the Klingon viewer tape
    d. none of the above

226) Who officiated over the ceremony in "Amok Time"?

227) What message did Trelane originally send the *Enterprise* in "Squire of Gothos"?
    a. Hip-Hip-Hurrah. Tally ho!
    b. Greetings, Earth Creatures!
    c. Hurrah!
    d. none of the above

228) What actor portrayed Samuel T. Cogley in "Court-Martial"?

. . . Answers

222. Laura Wood

223. b

224. Jackson Roykirk

225. b

226. T'Pau

227. a

228. Elisha Cook, Jr.

229) Kodos had once been governor of what planet in "Conscience of the King"?

230) In *Star Trek III*, what did Scotty sabotage on the *Excelsior*?

231) What character in "What Are Little Girls Made Of", was considered "the Pasteur of Archeological medicine"?

232) What actress portrayed Eleen in "Friday's Child"?

233) What does the Cloud Creature lose when it saves the Commissioner's life in "Metamorphosis"?

234) On the planet in "Cats Paw", Kirk encounters how many witches?

235) *Star Trek III* opened in _____ theatres across the United States and Canada on June 1, 1984.
    a. 627
    b. 1092
    c. 1692
    d. 1966

236) What character does Kirk fall in love with in "City On The Edge Of Forever"?

237) The plane visited in "Paradise Syndrome" is being threatened by a collision with what?

. . . *Answers*

229. Tarsus IV

230. The main transwarp computer drive

231. Dr. Roger Korby

232. Julie Newmar

233. Immortality

234. Three

235. d

236. Edith Keeler

237. Asteroid

238) In what Cary Grant movie does George Takei appear?

    a. *Notorious*
    b. *Walk, Don't Run*
    c. *His Girl Friday*
    d. *Kiss Them For Me*

239) *Gary Seven is immune to the Vulcan Nerve Pinch. True or false?*

240) *In "Patterns of Force", Gill was sent to the planet as a disciplinary observer. True or false?*

241) *The aliens in "By Any Other Name" were from what planet?*

242) *The U.S.S. Grissom* broadcasts of subspace radio frequency _____.

    a. 96.8
    b. 98.8
    c. 99.6
    d. 89.6

243) Fatigue and depression were the two major effects of the virus in "Immunity Syndrome". True or false?

244) What was the name of the Master Thrall in "Gamesters of Triskelion"?

245) In "Journey to Babel", how long are the fangs on a Sehlet?

. . . Answers

238. b

239. True

240. False

241. Kelva

242. b

243. True

244. Galt

245. 6 inch

QUESTIONS

246) The wreckage of what Federation vessel is discovered in "Bread and Circuses"?

247) Where is the *Enterprise* sent in "Trouble With Tribbles", to protect an important grain shipment?

248) Uhura tells the android in "I, Mudd" that she hopes it can provide her with eternal beauty and immortality. True or false?

249) Yeoman Rand became the obsessive desire of young Charlie in what episode?

250) What colors are the holographic airplanes in the "video game" shown in the bar sequence in *Star Trek III?*
    a. red and green
    b. red and yellow
    c. blue and yellow
    d. blue and green

251) Deela and boyfriend Raal tried to freeze the crew of the *Enterprise* in "Wink Of An Eye" for what purpose?

252) What was the name of Khan's ship in "Space Seed"?

253) In "Taste of Armageddon", "casualties" were asked to enter what chambers?

254) What actress portrayed Leila in "This Side of Paradise"?

. . . *Answers*

246. SS *Beagle*

247. Space Station-K7

248. True

249. "Charlie X"

250. a

251. Breeding

252. *Botany Bay*

253. Antimatter chambers

254. Jill Ireland

255) How does Spock discover the reason for creatures killing humans in "Devil in the Dark"?

256) In "Mark of Gideon", what is the name of the viral disease Kirk carries in his blood?

257) What did the transporter operator's autopsy show as the cause of death in "That Which Survives"?

258) What is the name of the Klingon commander in "Day of the Dove"?

259) In "Is There No Truth In Beauty", Jane's dress is a "complex _____ web".

260) What was the name of the scientific expedition in "The Children Shall Lead"?

261) Kirk must retrieve what from the government base in "Tomorrow Is Yesterday"?

262) In "Mudd's Women", what was the name of the "miracle drug" Mudd wanted Eve to take?

263) What is the name of Captain Kirk's starship in the TV series?

264) What actor originally portrayed Dr. Sulu?

265) What STAR TREK actor starred in the TV series, TEMPLE HOUSTON, 1963–64?

. . . *Answers*

255. Vulcan Mind Meld

256. Vegan Choriomeningitis

257. Cellular disruption

258. Kang

259. Sensor

260. Starnes

261. Film

262. Venus drug

263. USS *Enterprise*

264. George Takei

265. Jeffrey Hunter

266) "If transmissions are being monitored during battle, no uncoded messages on an open channel" is what regulation as told in *Star Trek II*?

267) What actress portrayed Zarabeth in "All Our Yesterdays"?

268) What is the real character name of the brilliant leader of the idealists in "Way to Eden"?

269) General Order #1, the Prime Directive means,
    a. self-destruct
    b. search
    c. noninterference
    d. doomsday

270) Who portrayed Dr. Robert Johnson in "Deadly Years"?

271) Which STAR TREK character wore a beard in "Mirror, Mirror"?

272) What year was the probe launched in "The Changeling"?

273) The destructive weapon in "Doomsday" was called a planet _____.

274) In "Amok Time", Spock's betrothed bride's name is _____.

. . . Answers

266. Regulation 46-A

267. Mariette Hartley

268. Dr. Sevrin

269. c

270. Felix Locker

271. Spock

272. 2020

273. Killer

274. T'Pring

275) What did the captured crew discover about the food they were served in "Squire of Gothos"?

    a. It was poisoned

    b. It was tasteless

    c. It was too hot

    d. It was very spicy

276) What was Captain Pike's first name in "The Menagerie"?

277) What episode marked the last appearance of Yeoman Rand in the STAR TREK TV series?

278) What STAR TREK character was Dr. Korby's fiancee?

279) What actor portrayed Kras in "Friday's Child"?

280) Cochane decided to leave the planet at the end of "Metamorphosis". True or false?

281) What two crewmen were turned into zombies in "Cat's Paw"?

    a. Sulu and Scotty

    b. Kirk and Spock

    c. Sulu and Spock

    d. Kirk and Scotty

. . . *Answers*

275. b

276. Christopher

277. "Conscience Of The King"

278. Nurse Chapel

279. Tige Andrews

280. False

281. a

282) In "City on the Edge of Forever", Spock likens using primitive tools and material to using:

    a. "ancient Vulcan weapons"

    b. "stone knives and bearskins"

    c. "needles and thread"

    d. none of the above

283) Kirk is studying the writings on what object when he falls through the trap door in "Paradise Syndrome"?

284) What is the character name of Seven's young secretary in "Assignment: Earth"?

285) Gill had decided to imitate what political culture in "Patterns of Force"?

286) The Kelvans are from what galaxy in "By Any Other Name"?

287) Spock is successful in destroying the virus creature in "Immunity Syndrome". True or false?

288) The Providers resembled what body organ in "Gamesters of Triskelion"?

289) What actress portrayed Spock's mother in "Journey to Babel"?

290) Who was the commander of the Federation vessel wrecked in "Bread and Circuses"?

. . . Answers

282. b

283. Obelisk

284. Roberta Lincoln

285. Nazi Germany

286. Andromeda

287. True

288. Brain

289. Jane Wyatt

290. Captain Merik

291) What was the name of the wheatlike grain the *Enterprise* crew must protect in "Trouble With Tribbles"?

292) What actor portrayed Norman in "I, Mudd"?

293) "This Side of Paradise" was an episode that told the story of colonists flooded by what rays?
   a. Darban
   b. X
   c. Berthold
   d. Sonic

294) The *Enterprise* auxiliary control is located where?
   a. Kirk's quarters
   b. Transporter Room
   c. The Landing Bay
   d. Engineering

295) The model used for Khan's vessel in "Space Seed" appears as what in "The Ultimate Computer"?

296) What Federation Ambassador accompanied the *Enterprise* in "Taste Of Armageddon"?

297) What STAR TREK actress was also Mrs. Charles Bronson?

298) What were the miners destroying that belonged to the Horta in "The Devil in the Dark"?

299) What was the name of Odona's father in "Mark of Gideon"?

. . . Answers

291. Quadrotriticale

292. Robert Tatro

293. c

294. d

295. Freighter

296. Robert Fox

297. Jill Ireland

298. Her eggs

299. Hodin

QUESTIONS

300) The planet was made of what substance in "That Which Survives"?

301) What was the name of Kang's wife in "Day of The Dove"?

302) What actress portrayed Jones in "Is There No Truth in Beauty"?

303) What is the name of the evil entity in "And The Children Shall Lead"?

304) What must Scotty duplicate in order to return the *Enterprise* in its own time frame in "Tomorrow Is Yesterday"?
    a. The slingshot effect
    b. The timewarp syndrome
    c. The timewarp effect
    d. none of the above

305 What actor portrayed Harry Mudd in the episode "Mudd's Women"?

306) "Beaming" was an effect created by Gene Roddenberry because the special effect needed to land a starship would have cost too much. True or false?

307) Captain Kirk's cabin was on what deck of the *Enterprise* in the TV series?
    a. 1   c. 5
    b. 3   d. 7

. . . Answers

300. Alloy of dyburneum osmyum

301. Mara

302. Diana Muldaur

303. Gorgan

304. a

305. Roger C. Carmel

306. True

307. c

308) The creatures surrounding Mr. Spock's casket in *Star Trek III* were originally _____ on the tube's surface.

309) Spock had never met Leila before she appeared in "This Side of Paradise". True or false?

310) Give the first name of the leader of the "supermen" in "Space Seed".

311) Who composed the music for "This Side of Paradise"?

312) In the TV series, what was the term used to describe as "fear of different life forms"?

313) Dr. McCoy's injection of an experimental drug in "City On The Edge of Forever", was intentional. True or false?

314) What was the name of the thief the *Enterprise* rescues in "Let This Be Your Last Battlefield"?
    a. LoKai
    b. John Robie
    c. Lusiera
    d. Jack The Ripper

315) What chemical gives the inhabitants in "Plato's Stepchildren" their power?

316) What actress portrayed Gem in "The Empath"?

. . . *Answers*

308. Microbes

309. False

310. Khan

311. Alexander Courage

312. Xenophobia

313. False

314. a

315. Kironide

316. Kathryn Hayes

317) In what episode did William Shatner's daughters appear?

318) Kirk responded "that should be just about right" when told he would be imprisoned for how many years in "Tomorrow Is Yesterday"?

319) What planet does the *Enterprise* visit in "The Man Trap"?

320) V'ger's probe was programmed to "observe and _____" the normal functions of the carbon-based units in *Star Trek: The Motion Picture*.
   a. challenge
   b. monitor
   c. record
   d. none of the above

321) Who was the captain of the *Reliant* before Khan took it over in *Star Trek II*?

322) DeForest Kelly co-starred as a villain in the movie *The Way West* with John Wayne. True or false?

323) Who was jokingly referred to as "The Great Bird of the Galaxy" by cast members of the STAR TREK series?

324) What book does Spock give Kirk as a birthday present in *Star Trek II*?

. . . Answers

317. "Miri"

318. 200

319. M-113

320. c

321. Captain Terrill

322. False

323. Gene Roddenberry

324. *Tale of Two Cities*

325) Flint was really Leonardo da Vinci, Johannes Brahms and several others throughout history in "Requiem For Methuseulah". True or false?

326) What is the name of the lieutenant supervising the transfer of new equipment in "Lights of Zetar"?

327) What was the actual age of character Robert Johnson in "Deadly Years"?

328) Who supplied the voice for Nomad in "The Changeling"?

329) Scotty is accused of _____ in "Wolf In The Fold".

330) What actress portrayed T'Pring in "Amok Time"?

331) Both aliens in "The Alternate Factor" share the same name. True or false?

332) When the *Enterprise* had first visited the Talosians Captain Kirk was in command. True or false?

333) T'Lar calls Sarek's request for Fal Tor Pan in *Star Trek III*, logical. True or false?

334) What actor portrayed Kodos/Koridian in "Conscience of The King"?

335) The Vulcan Mind Meld was first seen in the episode "Dagger of the Mind". True or false?

. . . Answers

325. True

326. Mira Romaine

327. 29

328. Vic Perrin

329. Murder

330. Arlene Martel

331. True

332. False

333. False

334. Arnold Moss

335. True

336) In "Who Mourns for Adonais", the god shows what female crew member too much attention?

337) STAR TREK actress Elinor Donahue portrayed what character in *Father Knows Best*?

338) Scotty and Sulu were returned to normal at the end of "Cat's Paw". True or false?

339) Marcy Lafferty Shatner portrayed what character in *Star Trek: The Motion Picture*?

340) What actor/announcer is the voice of the Guardian in "City On the Edge Of Forever"?

341) How many Romulan ships surround the *Enterprise* in "The Enterprise Incident"?

342) The *Enterprise* crew encounter a diamond shaped boundary marker in "Spectre of a Gun". True or false?

343) Name the computer breakthrough Daystrom had developed years previously in "Ultimate Computer".

344) What actor portrayed Rojan in "By Any Other Name"?

345) What was the name of the planet in "Piece Of The Action"?

... *Answers*

336. Lt. Carolyn Palamas

337. Betty (Princess) Anderson

338. True

339. Chief DeFalco

340. Bartel L. LaRue

341. Three

342. False

343. The Duotronic Breakthrough

344. Warren Stevens

345. Iotia

QUESTIONS

346) How many years had passed since Captain Garrovick's death and his son's encounter with the creature in "Obsession"?

347) What is the name of the tribal leader in "A Private Little War"?

348) There were no humans aboard the *Enterprise* when it was destroyed. True or false?

349) Both Spock's mother and father are Vulcans. True or false?

350) Jones was a dealer in rare commodities in "Trouble with Tribbles". True or false?

351) When was the first time a space docking was seen?

352) What was Dr. Piper's first name?
   a. Jim
   b. Bob
   c. Mark
   d. Steven

353) Spock was sprayed with what in "This Side of Paradise"?

354) What was Khan's full name in "Space Seed"?

355) Name the woman who wrote "This Side of Paradise".

. . . Answers

346. Eleven years

347. Tyree

348. True

349. False

350. True

351. *Star Trek: The Motion Picture*

352. c

353. Spores

354. Khan Noonian Singh

355. D.C. Fontana

356) What planet is visited in "Errand of Mercy"?

357) What does Mr. Spock sense from V'ger in *Star Trek: The Motion Picture*?
    a. Illogic
    b. Pure Logic
    c. Emotion
    d. none of the above.

358) The *Enterprise* was investigating what strange effects on the planet in "City On The Edge of Forever"?
    a. Intense Heat
    b. Planetary War
    c. Ripples in time
    d. None of the above

359) Lokai is a native of what planet?

360) By the end of "Plato's Stepchildren" Alexander develops the same powers as the Platonians. True or false?

361) What starship does the *Enterprise* find adrift in "Tholian Web"?

362) What was stolen in "Spock's Brain"?

363) Captain Christopher expressed a desire to become an astronaut and was planning on entering the astronaut training program. True or false?

. . . Answers

356. Organia

357. b

358. c

359. Cheron

360. False

361. USS *Defiant*

362. Spock's brain

363. False

364) William Shatner continued to act in *T.J. Hooker* while production was under way for *Star Trek III*. True or false?

365) What profession was Crater in "The Man Trap"?

366) What was the name stamped on the safety strap Chekov was holding on Ceti Alpha VI in *Star Trek II*?

367) What *Star Trek* actress is said to have been the first black woman to have a major role on television?

368) Samuel Peeple was the script writer used for the episode "Where No Man Has Gone Before". True or false?

369) Kirk quotes from his gift book in *Star Trek II*, "It was the best of times, it was the _____ _____ _____."

370) The reason Flint loses his mortality is because of his coming into contact with Kirk. True or false?

371) What planetoid houses the central library in the United Federation of Planets in "Lights of Zetar"?

372) What was the actual age of Elaine Johnson in "Deadly Years"?

373) What was Nomad's final fate in "The Changeling"?

. . . *Answers*

364. False

365. Archeology

366. SS *Botany Bay*

367. Nichelle Nichols

368. True

369. Worst of times

370. False

371. Memory Alpha

372. 27

373. Self-destruction

374) The victims of murder in "Wolf In The Fold" are men or women?

375) What actor portrayed Stonn in "Amok Time"?

376) There is only one way out for the trapped aliens in "Alternate Factor". True or false?

377) When Spock abducts him in "The Menagerie", Captain Pike is unable to respond to questions. True or false?

378) What actress portrayed Lenore Karidian in "Conscience of the King"?

379) What technique did Spock have to use to discover what had happened to Van Gelder in "Dagger of the Mind"?

380) Who is hurled through the air by a thunderbolt from Apollo in "Who Mourns For Adonais"?

381) Mr. Spock's curiosity got the better of him in "Metamorphosis" when he decided to touch the cloud creature. True or false?

382) What actor portrayed Korob in "Cat's Paw"?

383) What New York bridge is featured throughout "City On The Edge Of Forever"?

. . . Answers

374. Women

375. Lawrence Montaigne

376. False

377. False

378. Barbara Anderson

379. Vulcan Mind Meld

380. Scotty

381. True

382. Theo Marcuse

383. Brooklyn Bridge

384) What secret device do the Romulans have in "The Enterprise Incident"?

385) What famous "gunfight" is to be re-enacted in "Spectre of the Gun"?

386) What is the name of the commodore who leads the squadron of starships in practice maneuvers against the *Enterprise* in "The Ultimate Computer"?

387) What *Star Trek* actor portrayed Dr. Ostrow in "Forbidden Planet"?

388) What was the name of the book left on the planet in "A Piece of The Action"?

389) What rank was Captain Garrovick's son in "Obsession"?

390) Kirk is bitten by what in "A Private Little War"?

391) What is Spock's father's name?

392) The name of the "fluffballs" brought to the space station by Jones in "The Trouble With Tribbles" were called tribbles. True or false?

. . . Answers

384. Cloaking device

385. OK Corral

386. Robert Wesley

387. Warren Stevens

388. *Chicago Mobs Of The Twenties*

389. Ensign

390. Mugatu

391. Sarek

392. True

393) Why did Kirk leave the *Enterprise*'s shields down in the "Ultimate Computer"?

    a. They weren't working properly

    b. To make the other starships back off from their attack

    c. To test the mettle of his crew

    d. None of the above.

394) Cast Rodinum is a metal that was used in the "Neutral Zone Earth" outposts for what purpose?

    a. fences

    b. doors

    c. shields

    d. spacedock

395) Spock's Vulcan father's name was

    a. Saron

    b. Salabok

    c. Sarek

    d. Spock

396) Who discovers the antidote in "This Side of Paradise"?

397) In "Space Seed", Khan was a product of selective breeding from what decade in Earth history?

398) Spock beams down to the planet in his Federation uniform, but halfway through changes into a colony uniform in "This Side of Paradise". True or false?

. . . Answers

393. b

394. c

395. c

396. Kirk

397. 1990's

398. True

399) How many men made up the Organian Council in "Errand of Mercy"?

400) What was the name of the "living machine" in "City On The Edge Of Forever"?

401) What are Mr. Spock's first words after he is revived?
   a. "My father says that you have been my friend".
   b. "Jim, your name is Jim."
   c. "The needs of the one outweighed the needs of the other."
   d. "Jim, I have been and ever shall be your friend."

402) What is the name of the chief officer of political traitors in "Let This Be Your Last Battlefield"?

403) What actor portrayed Alexander in "Plato's Stepchildren"?

404) Who is stranded aboard the drifting starship when it vanishes in "Tholian Web"?

405) Kirk follows the Alien to what numbered planet in the system in "Spock's Brain"?

406) Kirk told Captain Christopher to take a good look around, as he had "made it out here ahead of them all" in "Tomorrow Is Yesterday". True or false?

. . . Answers

399. Three

400. Guardian of Forever

401. a

402. Bele

403. Michael Dunn

404. Kirk

405. Sixth

406. True

407) What was Crater's wife's first name in "The Man Trap"?

408) In 1952, what actor appeared as Narab, the alien in "Zombies Of The Stratosphere"?

409) In "This Side of Paradise", what is Mr. Spock's explanation for not telling humans his first name.
    a. they wouldn't like the sound of it.
    b. they wouldn't know how to pronounce it
    c. it is too difficult to spell
    d. none of the above.

410) What STAR TREK actress developed the company "Women in Motion" which helped to attract women and minorities to the Space Program?

411) Who was the first computer to write music for STAR TREK?

412) The final budget for *Star Trek: The Motion Picture* was closest to which of the following figures?
    a. 5 million dollars
    b. 15 million dollars
    c. 25 million dollars
    d. 35 million dollars

413) What substitute for glasses is Kirk allergic to in *Star Trek II*?

414) What is the name of Flint's beautiful ward in "Requiem For Methuselah?

. . . Answers

407. Nancy

408. Leonard Nimoy

409. b

410. Nichelle Nichols

411. Alexander Courage

412. d

413. Retinox 5

414. Reena Kapec

415) Which of the *Enterprise* crew is romantically involved with Mira in "Lights of Zetar"?

416) What old friend of Kirk's aids McCoy in the search for an antidote in "Deadly Years"?

417) The rocks explode in "The Apple". True or false?

418) What Earth name is given the real murderer in "Wolf In The Fold"?

419) Who created/designed the wardrobe for "Amok Time"?

420) The aliens were trapped in a corridor between both their universes in "Alternate Factor". True or false?

421) What was Sulu's "new toy" he discovered in "Shore Leave"?

422) On what planet did the *Enterprise* shuttle craft crash land in "Galileo Seven"?

423) Name the psychiatrist who accompanied Kirk in "Dagger of the Mind".

424) In "Who Mourns For Adonais", what is the god's power source?
    a. his hand   d. none of the above
    b. the temple
    c. his headdress

. . . *Answers*

415. Mr. Scott

416. Dr. Janice Wallace

417. True

418. Jack The Ripper

419. William Theiss

420. True

421. Police Special Pistol

422. Taursus II

423. Dr. Helen Noel

424. b

425) Who wrote "Friday's Child"?

426) What actress portrayed Sylvia in "Cat's Paw"?

427) What actor portrayed Rodent in "City On The Edge of Forever"?

428) Spock's reply to Saavik's astonishment that Kirk is so "human" in *Star Trek II*, is "Nobody's _____."

429) Who is responsible for the *Enterprise* crew being transported to the "wild west town" in "Spectre of the Gun"?

430) What actor portrayed Daystrom in "The Ultimate Computer"?

431) What did Kirk say was a form of apology in "By Any Other Name"?

432) In what year had the book left on the planet in "Piece of the Action" been published?

433) On what planet does the *Enterprise* landing party encounter a cloudlike creature in "Obsession"?

434) Name the character who cures Kirk in "Private Little War".

435) What is Spock's mother's name?

. . . Answers

425. D.C. Fontana

426. Antoinette Bower

427. John Harmon

428. Perfect

429. Melkots

430. William Marshall

431. Kissing

432. 1992

433. Argus X

434. Nona

435. Amanda

436) What was put in the grain bins, in "Trouble With Tribbles"?

437) "The Alternate Factor" episode mentions which Starbase?
    a. 100
    b. 200
    c. 300
    d. 400

438) Doc's sickbay was a torture chamber in which episode?

439) Khan is given the choice of colonization or _____-_____ in "Space Seed".

440) What actor portrayed Tamar in "Return of The Archons"?

441) The Organians were creatures of pure _____.

442) McCoy vanishes into what planet's past in "City On The Edge Of Forever"?

443) Who does Captain Kirk leave in command of the *Enterprise* when he leaves the *Enterprise*, on foot, to inspect V'ger?
    a. Mr. Scott
    b. Mr. Sulu
    c. Lieutenant Uhura
    d. Mr. Chekov

. . . *Answers*

436. Poison

437. b

438. "Mirror, Mirror"

439. Court-martial

440. Jon Lormer

441. Energy

442. Earth

443. b

444) What planet houses an insane asylum in "Whom Gods Destroy"?

445) What planet sends a distress call in "Wink of an Eye"?

446) What major TV award did "The Tholian Web" win for STAR TREK?

447) Spock's voice is heard over Chekov's communicator in "Spock's Brain". True or false?

448) Who inspects the *Enterprise* on its return to starbase?
     a. Captain Styles
     b. Commander Morrow
     c. Admiral Nogura
     d. Admiral Kirk

449) How long does the orgy last in "Return of the Archons"?

450) What was the creature in "The Man Trap" able to change?
     a. time
     b. its shape
     c. its spots
     d. none of the above

. . . Answers

444. Elba II

445. Scalos

446. Emmy

447. False

448. b

449. One hour

450. b

QUESTIONS

451) Space Station _____ warns the Federation about V'ger in STAR TREK: The Motion Picture.
   a. Epsilon 9
   b. Delta 5
   c. Omicron 3
   d. Omega 4

452) What *Star Trek* actor wrote "You and I", a book containing beautiful photographs and poetry?

453) The Ceti Eel wraps itself around what part of the brain in *Star Trek II*?

454) Alien creatures of Deneva were finally killed in "Operation Annililate" by
   a. phasers set on force 3
   b. Berium radiation
   c. temperatures of 9000F
   d. Ultra violet light

455) William Shatner had never appeared in a television series prior to *Star Trek*. True or false?

456) Lieutenant Saavik in *Star Trek II*, feels that humor is a "difficult _____."

457) What famous man is seen outside the *Enterprise* and asks to be beamed aboard in "Savage Curtain"?

458) A rare element is needed to stop a plague on what planet in "Cloudminders"?

. . . Answers

451. a

452. Leonard Nimoy

453. Cerebral Cortex

454. d

455. False

456. Concept

457. Abraham Lincoln

458. Merak II

459) What "tried and true" bluff did Kirk use to save the *Enterprise* in "Deadly Years"?

460) What is the name of the "high priest" in "The Apple"?

461) The author of "Wolf In The Fold" is best known for what classic novel, written in 1957?

462) What was Decker's rank in "Doomsday"?

463) What was the name of the pilot captured by the *Enterprise* tractor beam in "Tomorrow Is Yesterday"?

464) Who supposedly "kills" Dr. McCoy in "Shore Leave"?

465) What game did Spock play against the computer to test its memory in "Court-Martial"?

466) What actor who appeared in "Dagger of the Mind" also portrayed character "Punk" in the TV series *Dallas*?

467) Who wrote "Amok Time"?

468) What is the title of the leader in "Friday's Child"?

469) The shuttlecraft is drawn off course to what planet in "Metamorphosis"?

. . . Answers

459. Corbomite

460. Akuta

461. *Psycho*

462. Commodore

463. Capt. John Christopher

464. Black knight

465. Chess

466. Morgan Woodward

467. Theodore Sturgeon

468. High Teer

469. Gamma Canaris

470) Kirk discovers his brother is dead in "Operation: Annihilate". True or false?

471) If Keeler is allowed to live, what country would win World War II, in "City On The Edge Of Forever"?

472) What two planets are at war in "Elaan of Troyius"?

473) The *Enterprise* crew beams down to what planet in "Omega Glory"?

474) What alien inhabits Spock's body in "Return to Tomorrow"?

475) What does McCoy leave behind in "Piece of the Action"?

476) What is the creature's native plane in "Obsession"?

477) What is the name of the doctor who treats Spock on board the *Enterprise* in "Private Little War"?

478) Sarek is suffering from heart problems in "Journey to Babel". True or false?

479) Where does Scotty send the *Enterprise*'s tribbles in "Trouble With Tribbles"?

. . . Answers

470. True

471. Germany

472. Elas, Troyius

473. Omega IV

474. Henock

475. Communicator

476. Tycho IV

477. Dr. M'Benga

478. True

479. Klingon battle cruiser

480) In the "City On The Edge of Forever", McCoy arrived in what city?
   a. New York City
   b. Chicago
   c. Los Angeles
   d. Detroit

481) Dr. Daystrom created a multiplex computer named Albert in "The Ultimate Computer". True or false?

482) What was the historian's full name in "Space Seed"?

483) What actor portrayed Marplon in "Return of The Archons"?

484) Kirk organizes a commando raid on the Klingons' ammunitions dump in "Errand of Mercy". True or false?

485) Kirk and Spock find themselves in New York City in what year in "City On The Edge of Forever"?

486) Mr. Spock's quarters in *Star Trek III* are located on which deck?
   a. deck 5
   b. deck 7
   c. C deck
   d. D deck

. . . Answers

480. a

481. False

482. Marla McGivers

483. Torin Thatcher

484. True

485. 1930

486. c

487) What was the name of the colony's governor in "Whom Gods Destroy"?

488) What does Kirk drink in "Wink of An Eye" that accelerates him to another level?

489) What is the name of the planet in "The World Is Hollow And I Have Touched The Sky"?

490) What is the name of the entity encased in a protective chamber in "Is There No Truth In Beauty"?

491) What was Reger's daughter's name in "Return of the Archons"?

492) In what episode does the *Enterprise* first travel through time?

493) William Shatner appeared briefly as the dead body of Sam Kirk in the episode "Operation: Annihilate". True or false?

494) Admiral Kirk claims he likes inspections in *Star Trek II*. True or false?

495) Complete this line of dialog from "Operation: Annihilate" "Tis a pity brief blindness did not increase your appreciation of _____."

496) Who starred in the TWILIGHT ZONE episodes "Nick of Time" and "Nightmare at 20,000 Feet"?

. . . Answers

487. Donald Cory

488. Scalosian water

489. Yonada

490. Kolos

491. Tula

492. "Naked Time"

493. True

494. False

495. Beauty

496. William Shatner

QUESTIONS

497) What is the name of the illegal ale McCoy gives Kirk on his birthday in *Star Trek II*?

498) What is the name of the legendary Vulcan peacemaker seen in "Savage Curtain"?
   a. Sarek
   b. Spock
   c. Surak
   d. Kirock

499) What are the miners called in "Cloudminders"?

500) Mr. Spock is not affected by the aging process in "Deadly Years". True or false?

501) What does the *Enterprise* use to destroy Vaal in "The Apple"?

502) What actor portrayed Hengist in "Wolf in The Fold"?

503) Who was the only crewman found on board the *Constellation* in "Doomsday"?

504) What was Daystrom's computer breakthrough, "claim to fame" in "The Ultimate Computer"?

505) Dr. McCoy saw a giant white rabbit in "Shore Leave". True or false?

506) What was the name of the records officer apparently inside the jettisoned pod in "Court-Martial"?

. . . *Answers*

497. Romulan

498. c

499. Troglytes

500. False

501. Phasers

502. John Fiedler

503. Decker

504. Duotronic breakthrough in computer technology

505. True

506. Ben Finney

QUESTIONS

507) What actress portrayed Miri?

508) What is the name for the Vulcan mating cycle?

509) What visiting Klingon character interferes with Kirk and the planet's inhabitants in "Friday's Child"?

510) What is the name of the castaway discovered on the planet surface in "Metamorphosis"?

511) What was Kirk's relationship to Peter in "Operation: Annihilate".
    a. Kirk's brother
    b. Kirk's son
    c. Kirk's nephew
    d. none of the above.

512) In order for history to restore itself in "City On The Edge of Forever", what must happen to Keeler?

513) What is Elaan's title in "Elaan of Troyius"?

514) What was the name of the starship captain discovered on the planet surface in "Omega Glory"?

515) Which alien inhabits Mulhall's body in "Return to Tomorrow"?

516) What was the slang term used for a gun in "Piece of The Action"?

. . . Answers

507. Kim Darby

508. Pon Far

509. Kras

510. Zephram Cochrane

511. c

512. Die

513. Dohlman of Elas

514. Ronald Tracey

515. Thalassa

516. Heater

517) Spock discovers the creature is intelligent in "Obsession" because it decides to turn and fight. True or false?

518) What actor portrayed Dr. M'Benga in "Private Little War"?

519) *Star Trek: The Motion Picture* grossed _____ in its first weekend of national release?
    a. 5.2 million dollars
    b. 8.3 million dollars
    c. 11.8 million dollars
    d. 14.3 million dollars

520) Who is called upon to donate blood to Saren in "Journey to Babel"?

521) The title of the episode "Who Mourns for Adonais" is a Shakespearean quote. True or false?

522) Kirk became the new medicine man in "The Paradise Syndrome". True or false?

523) What actor portrayed Khan in "Space Seed"?

524) Actor Jon Lorimer portrayed four different characters in four different *Star Trek* episodes. True or false?

525) "Errand of Mercy" director John Newland, created the syndicated series *One Step Beyond*. True or false?

. . . *Answers*

517. True

518. Booker Marshall

519. c

520. Spock

521. False

522. True

523. Ricardo Montalban

524. False

525. True

526) The action in "Devil in the Dark" took place on what planet?

527) What was the name of the former starship captain who became an inmate in "Whom Gods Destroy"?

528) Dr. McCoy told Admiral Kirk to "climb the steps of _____ _____" in *Star Trek III*.

529) What is the name of the Queen of Scalos in "Wink of An Eye"?

530) The planet in "The World Is Hollow And I Have Touched the Sky" is actually a spherical spaceship. True or false?

531) Kolos, in "Is There No Truth In Beauty," is of what race?

532) What was the name of the orgy in "Return of the Archons"?

533) Mr. Sulu is seen bare chested, carrying a sword in the episode "Naked Time". True or false?

534) Captain Kirk was the only member of his family to call his brother Sam. True or false?

535) Who is the captain of the *Enterprise* in *Star Trek II*?

. . . *Answers*

526. Janus VI

527. Garth of Izar

528. Mt. Seleya

529. Deela

530. True

531. Medusan

532. The Red Hour

533. True

534. True

535. Spock

536) In *Star Trek: The Motion Picture*, V'ger purposefully prevented reception of the transmit code because it wished to
    a. replenish its power reserves
    b. meet its creator "in person"
    c. both of the above
    d. none of the above

537) In 1964, William Shatner was cast as Assistant District Attorney in the TV series *For The People*. True or false?

538) What is the name of Dr. Marcus' Spacelab in *Star Trek II*?

539) What disease-free planet does Kirk beam down to in "Mark of Gideon"?

540) What is the name of the city that floats above the planet in "Cloudminders"?

541) What actress portrayed Dr. Wallace in "Deadly Years"?

542) Vaal was a computer constructed in the "dim time". True or false?

543) Lt. Saavik and David Marcus pick up radiation readings from Mr. Spock's casket in *Star Trek III*. True or false?

. . . *Answers*

536. b

537. True

538. Regula I

539. Gideon

540. Stratos

541. Sarah Marshall

542. True

543. True

QUESTIONS

544) What actor portrayed Morla in "Wolf In The Fold"?

545) Decker transported his entire crew to the planet destroyed in "Doomsday Machine". True or false?

546) How many years had passed since Daystrom made history with a computer breakthrough in "Ultimate Computer"?

547) Finnegan's uniform in "Shore Leave" is minus an Academy Cadet emblem. True or false?

548) Name the prosecuting attorney in "Court-Martial".

549) The children in "Miri" were part of a life-prolongation experiment. True or false?

550) In what episode do the Romulans make their first appearance?

551) What was the character name of the deposed leader in "Friday's Child"?

552) The *Enterprise* is rated "fully operational" after the run-in with V'ger in *Star Trek: The Motion Picture*. True or false?

553) In "Metamorphosis", Cochrane is the scientist who discovered what 100 years previously?

. . . *Answers*

544. Charles Dierkop

545. True

546. 25

547. False

548. Areel Shaw

549. True

550. "Balance of Terror"

551. Akaar

552. True

553. Space Warp Drive

554) Spock is temporarily what in "Operation: Annihilate"?

555) How does Kirk's social worker/girl friend die in "City On The Edge Of Forever"?

556) Complete Mr. Spock's line of dialog from "Trouble With Tribbles". "He heard you. He simply could not believe his _____."

557) What is the name of the Troyian ambassador in "Elaan of Troyius"?

558) What is the name of the "oriental" looking rulers in "Omega Glory"?

559) Dr. McCoy is concerned about the "high _____ rate" required for "possession" in "Return to Tomorrow".

560) What card game does Kirk invent in "Piece of The Action"?

561) The U.S.S. *Grissom* was named in honor of American astronaut Gus Grissom. True or false?

562) In whose quarters does the creature enter the ship in "Obsession"?

563) What actress portrayed Nona in "Private Little War"?

. . . Answers

554. Blinded

555. Traffic accident

556. Ears

557. Petri

558. Kohms

559. Metabolic

560. Fizzbin

561. True

562. Garrovick's

563. Nancy Kovack

564) What character stabs Kirk in "Journey to Babel"?

565) Mr. Scott decides to fight the Klingons after they insult his beloved _____, in "Trouble With Tribbles".

566) The Elaasian Ambassador in "Elaan of Troyuis" was called what?
- a. Sarek
- b. Petri
- c. Bilar
- d. Mara

567) Kirk discovered violent emotions cured the effects of the spores in "This Side of Paradise". True or false?

568) What was McGivers' official crew assignment on the *Enterprise*, in "Space Seed"?

569) What actor portrayed Reger in "Return Of The Archons"?

570) Name the Klingon commander in "Errand of Mercy".

571) James Horner composed the music for *Star Trek: The Motion Picture*. True or false?

572) Who is the first to leap through the past in "City On The Edge of Forever"?

573) What two colors made up the Cheron feuders in "Let This Be Your Last Battlefield"?

. . . Answers

564. Thelev

565. *Enterprise*

566. b

567. True

568. Historian

569. Harry Townes

570. Kor

571. False

572. Dr. McCoy

573. Black and White

574) *Star Trek* was the first network television show to feature an inter-racial kiss. True or false?

575) What alien race wove an energy web around the *Enterprise* in "Tholian Web"?

576) Kirk follows the alien to what system in "Spock's Brain"?

577) Who is the youngster who asks Kirk if they will receive a hero's welcome upon their return in *Star Trek III*.
- a. Trainee Foster
- b. Trainee Igo
- c. Lieutenant Singer
- d. Trainee Moruzzi

578) What actor portrayed Captain Christopher in "Tomorrow Is Yesterday"?

579) What is Crater's first name in "The Man Trap"?

580) Leonard Nimoy portrayed a soldier unconvinced of reports that giant ants were threatening mankind in the movie
- a. *Them*
- b. *Terror of the Ants*
- c. *Chosen*
- d. *The Awful Truth*

581) How many of Khan's people are claimed to have been sent into exile by Kirk in *Star Trek II*?

. . . Answers

574. True

575. Tholians

576. Sigma Draconis

577. a

578. Roger Perry

579. Robert

580. a

581. 70

582) What actress portrayed Number One in the original pilot episode?

583) STAR TREK became the first TV series in the history of television to provide two pilot episodes to the network. True or false?

584) Complete this line of dialog by Carol Marcus in *Star Trek II*. "Jim Kirk was many things but he was never a _____ _____."

585) In "Requiem For Methuselah", Reena dies because of a fight between Flint and Dr. McCoy. True or false?

586) The last inhabitants of what planet take over Mira's body in "Lights Of Zetar"?

587) The commodore on board the *Enterprise* was enroute to what starbase in "Deadly Years"?

588) What planet does the *Enterprise* crew visit in "Apple"?

589) Mr. Spock describes V'ger as a _____ in *Star Trek: The Motion Picture*.
    a. god
    b. child
    c. carbon unit
    d. none of the above

. . . Answers

582. Majel Barrett

583. True

584. Boy scout

585. False

586. Zetar

587. 10

588. Gamma Trianguli VI

589. b

590) When the entity is trapped in "Wolf In The Fold", what character is it masquerading as?

591) What STAR TREK actor made the phrase "rich, Corinthian leather" famous for Chrysler?

592) What actor portrayed Admiral Komach in "Amok Time"?

593) What actor portrayed Lazarus in "The Alternate Factor"?

594) What was the name of Kirk's old academy "enemy" he meets up with in "Shore Leave"?

595) What was the name of the *Enterprise* shuttlecraft in "Galileo Seven"?

596) What device was used to alter Van Gelder's mind in "Dagger of the Mind"?

597) What actor portrayed Apollo in "Who Mourns For Adonais"?

598) What planet is visited in the episode "Friday's Child"?

599) What, besides Kirk, McCoy and Spock, is chained to the wall in "Cat's Paw"?

600) Lieutenant Ilia, in *Star Trek: The Motion Picture*, is from the what planet?

. . . *Answers*

590. Administrator Hengist

591. Ricardo Montalban

592. Byron Morrow

593. Robert Brown

594. Finnegan

595. Galileo

596. Neutral neutralizer

597. Michael Forest

598. Capella IV

599. A skeleton

600. Delta

601) In what episode besides "City On The Edge of Forever" did the actor portraying Rodent appear?

602) Captain Kirk supposedly suffers a "nervous breakdown" in "Enterprise Incident". True or false?

603) How many mind melds, total, does Spock perform on his fellow crewmen in "Spectre of The Gun"?

604) Who is referred to as "Captain Dunsel" in "The Ultimate Computer"?

605) In "Return to Tomorrow", Kirk delivers a speech citing man's historic landing on the moon, which aired prior to that event actually happening. True or false?

606) What gang leader first makes contact with the landing party in "Piece of The Action"?

607) What type of bomb is used to destroy the gaseous creature in "Obsession"?

608) Nona is murdered right after she demonstrates the phaser to the Hill People. True or false?

609) Spock's parents make their first appearance in which episode?

610) The death of Tribbles was what led to the discovery that the grain shipment had been tainted in "Trouble With Tribbles". True or false?

. . . Answers

601. "A Piece of the Action"

602. True

603. Three

604. Captain Kirk

605. True

606. Bela Oxmyx

607. Matter/antimatter

608. False (before)

609. "Journey To Babel"

610. True

611) After patching up the Horta, Dr. McCoy felt he could do what?

    a. cure all diseases
    b. cure a rainy day
    c. cure the common cold
    d. cure a headache

612) What were the names of the two starships in "The Doomsday Machine"?

613) Khan cuts off what to the bridge to take over the ship in "Space Seed"?

614) How many STAR TREK episodes exist, total?

615) The Federation is at odds with what Empire in "Errand of Mercy"?

616) As soon as McCoy leaps through the portal in "City On The Edge of Forever", what ship ceases to exist?

617) What famous impressionist is seen in "Let This Be Your Last Battlefield"?

618) What STAR TREK actor was once married to *I Dream of Jeannie* star, Barbara Eden?

619) The "forced" inter-racial kiss in "Plato's Stepchildren" was between what two characters?

. . . *Answers*

611. b

612. The *Enterprise*, The *Constellation*

613. Air (oxygen)

614. 79

615. Klingon

616. *Enterprise*

617. Frank Gorshin

618. Michael Ansara

619. Kirk, Uhura

620) What two crew members view Kirk's last will and testament in "Tholian Web"?

621) Mr. Spock achieves Kolinahr in *Star Trek: The Motion Picture*. True or false?

622) What was the name of the leader responsible for the theft in "Spock's Brain"?

623) Name the ship that disappeared in "Return of the Archons".

624) What was Mr. Sulu's hobby in "The Man Trap"?

625) Who appeared as a reporter covering the murder trial of Adam Zink, a robot, in "The Outerlimits episode I, Robot"?

626) How many months after Khan was exiled did he claim Ceti Alpha VI exploded in *Star Trek II*?

627) What STAR TREK actress was to become Mrs. Gene Roddenberry?

628) William Shatner and Leonard Nimoy had never worked together prior to STAR TREK. True or false?

629) In *Star Trek II*, when Kirk's party was cleared for docking, they were told to approach what area?

630) What does Mr. Spock say when "touching" Kirk's mind at the end of "Requiem For Methuselah"?

. . . Answers

620. Spock, McCoy

621. False

622. Kara

623. USS *Archon*

624. Botany

625. Leonard Nimoy

626. 6 months

627. Majel Barrett

628. False

629. Portside Torpedo Bay

630. Forget

631) What planet does the *Enterprise* journey to in "Cloudminders"?

632) What was the name of the commodore onboard the *Enterprise* in "Deadly Years"?

633) What do the people in "The Apple" call themselves?

634) What actor portrayed Admiral Kirk in *Star Trek II*?

635) What crippled starship does the *Enterprise* encounter in "Doomsday"?

636) The *Enterprise* is sent back in time to what century in "Tomorrow is Yesterday"?

637) What actor portrayed Finnegan in "Shore Leave"?

638) In what episode does the *Enterprise* shuttlecraft first appear?

639) What actor portrayed Dr. Adams in "Dagger of the Mind"?

640) What actress portrayed Palamos in "Who Mourns For Adonais"?

641) What is the name of the war-like inhabitants of the planet in "Friday's Child"?

. . . Answers

631. Ardana

632. George Stocker

633. Feeders of Vaal

634. William Shatner

635. USS *Constellation*

636. 20th

637. Bruce Mars

638. "Galileo 7"

639. James Gregory

640. Leslie Parrish

641. Capellans

642) The shuttlecraft is carrying what ailing character in "Metamorphosis"?

643) What planet is the home of Kirk's brother and family in "Operation: Annihilate"?

644) Spock uses vintage equipment to construct a *mnemonic* memory circuit in "City On The Edge of Forever". True or false?

645) Spock helps his crew accept the gunfight as "flesh and blood" reality in "Spectre of The Gun". True or false?

646) What term in "Ultimate Computer" means "a part serving no useful purpose"?

647) Which alien takes over Kirk's body in "Return to Tomorrow"?

648) Jojo _____ is one of the rival gangsters in "Piece of the Action".

649) What is in the jar used to bait the creature in "Obsession"?

650) By the end of "Private Little War", the *Enterprise* crew is able to negotiate a peaceful settlement to the war. True or false?

651) Sarek is the prime suspect in the murder of whom in "Journey To Babel"?

. . . *Answers*

642. Nancy Hedford

643. Deneva

644. True

645. False

646. Dunsel

647. Sargon

648. Krako

649. Blood

650. False

651. Ambassador Gav

652) Darvin is exposed as a what in "Trouble With Tribbles"?

653) What was the name of the ship's surgeon in "The Cage"?
    a. McCoy
    b. Boyce
    c. Hart
    d. Lewis

654) The Claymore used by Scotty in "The Day of The Dove" is what?
    a. Tool
    b. Sword
    c. Computer
    d. None of the above

655) Kirk releases anesthetic gas to recapture the *Enterprise* in "Space Seed". True or false?

656) Complete Dr. McCoy's line of dialog in "Return of The Archons". ". . . blessed be the body and health to all of its _____."

657) Kirk and McCoy go "undercover" in "Errand of Mercy". True or false?

658) Kirk and _____ follow McCoy through the portal in "City On The Edge of Forever".

. . . *Answers*

652. Klingon

653. b

654. b

655. True

656. Parts

657. False (Spock)

658. Spock

659) What actor portrayed Bele in "Let This Be Your Last Battlefield"?

660) McCoy and Spock lie to their captain in "Tholian Web" when they tell Kirk they did not get a chance to view his will. True or false?

661) What is the device McCoy uses to restore Spock's brain in "Spock's Brain"?

662) Name the planet visited by the *Enterprise* in "Return of the Archons"?

663) The entity in "The Man Trap" required what common compound to survive?

664) What STAR TREK actor was born in Boston, Massachusetts on March 26, 1931?

665) What creature killed Khan's wife, as noted in *Star Trek II*?

666) What was Nurse Chapel's first name?

667) The phaser rifle used in "Where No Man Has Gone Before" was used only three times during the series. True or false?

668) What was the name of Khan's creature/weapon in *Star Trek II*?

. . . *Answers*

659. Frank Gorshin

660. True

661. The teacher

662. Beta III

663. Salt (sodium chloride)

664. Leonard Nimoy

665. Ceti Eel

666. Christine

667. False (once)

668. Ceti Eel

QUESTIONS

669) What actor portrayed Flint in "Requiem For Methuselah"?

670) In Cloudminders," what rare element is found in great proportions on Ardana?

671) The shortcut suggested by the commodore in "Deadly Years" leads the *Enterprise* through what zone?

672) What is the name of the energy source in "The Apple"?

673) Who wrote "Wolf In The Fold"?

674) Who is the captain of the *Constellation* in "The Doomsday Machine"?

675) Give the serial number of the jet pilot captured by the *Enterprise* tractor beam in "Tomorrow is Yesterday"?

676) In "Shore Leave," the *Enterprise* crew discover the planet they are on is an _____ _____.

677) Spock provided a "distress flare" by jettisoning what, in "Galileo Seven"?

678) Who operated the transporter on the Klingon vessel in *Star Trek III*?

679) What actor portrayed Dr. VanGelder in "Dagger of the Mind"?

. . . Answers

669. James Daly

670. Zienite

671. Romulan Neutral Zone

672. Vaal

673. Robert Bloch

674. Matthew Decker

675. 4857932

676. Amusement park

677. Fuel

678. Maltz

679. Morgan Woodward

680) Who created the greek style gown seen in "Who Mourns For Adonais"?

681) What is the name of the deposed leader's wife in "Friday's Child"?

682) What is Hedford's title in "Metamorphosis"?

683) What is the epidemic affecting the planet in "Operation: Annihilate"?

684) What actor portrayed Sarek, Spock's father?

685) Whose voice is heard as the "warning buoy" in "Spectre of The Gun"?

686) The *Enterprise* discovers what starship in "Omega Glory"?

687) Kirk, McCoy and what other doctor are transported to the planet's underground in "Return To Tomorrow"?

688) V'ger is searching for its creator so that it can _____ its creator in *Star Trek: The Motion Picture*.
    a. destroy
    b. join with
    c. Both of the above
    d. None of the above

689) Who does Kirk say will want "a piece of the action", in "A Piece of The Action"?

. . . Answers

680. William Theiss

681. Eleen

682. Commissioner

683. Mass insanity

684. Mark Lenard

685. James Doohan

686. *Exeter*

687. Anne Mulhall

688. b

689. The Federation

690) Upon tasting whose copper-based blood does the creature flee in "Obsession"?

691) What episode, written by Gene Roddenberry, was inspired by the Vietnam War?

692) Gav is a _____ ambassador.

693) The tribbles like Klingons. True or false?

694) What actor portrayed Captain Christopher's son, Sean, in "Tomorrow is Yesterday".
    a. William Shatner
    b. Robert Foster
    c. Roger Perry
    d. None of the above

695) What is Mr. Scott's new title when he returns to starbase in *Star Trek III*?

696) Complete the title of this episode: "Devil In The _____".

697) Bela Oxmyx called Mr. Spock a "dope" in "Piece of the Action". True or false?

698) Starfleet planned to _____ the *Enterprise* upon its return to starbase.
    a. decommission
    b. scrap
    c. modify
    d. overhaul

. . . Answers

690. Spock's

691. "Private Little War"

692. Tellerite

693. False

694. d

695. Captain of Engineering

696. "Devil in The *Dark*"

697. True

698. a

699) From what planet was Elaan in "Elaan of Troyius"?

700) The Klingons controlled what decks in "Day of the Dove"?

701) The only time Edith Keeler is seen is in what episode?

702) What is Kirk's middle initial?

703) In "Space Seed", the *Botany Bay* was what class ship?
   a. DY100
   b. M-5
   c. DY300
   d. M

704) Complete this line, "Well, then thank _____ and pointed ears!"
   a. God
   b. starships
   c. green blood
   d. pitchforks

705) Dr. McCoy never said "I don't make housecalls". True or false?

. . . Answers

699. Elas

700. Deck 6, Starboard Deck7

701. "City On The Edge of Forever"

702. T

703. a

704. d

705. False

706) Who was told "Picturesque descriptions will not mend broken circuits".
   a. Mr. Spock
   b. Mr. Scott
   c. Dr. McCoy
   d. Capt. Kirk

707) In "Patterns of Force", Spock and Kirk use crystals from what to burn out the jail cell lock?
   a. transporter
   b. phasers
   c. transponders
   d. communicators

708) To what "city" was Kirk and crew sent in "Spectre of The Gun"?
   a. Virginia City
   b. Melkotia
   c. Tombstone
   d. Philadelphia

709) What does UESPA stand for?

710) Dr. Korby discovered what important technique?
   a. vulcanization
   b. immunization
   c. hypertension
   d. dissension

711) What kind of apples did Gary Mitchell like in "Where No Man Has Gone Before"?

. . . Answers

706. b

707. c

708. c

709. United Earth Space Probe Agency

710. b

711. Kafarian

712) How many sisters has Captain Kirk?

713) Where is Captain Kirk's command chair located?

714) What was Kirk's relationship to David in *Star Trek II?*
    a. father
    b. uncle
    c. brother
    d. stepfather

715) Mr. Spock has pointed ears. True or false?

716) What does Eleen in "Friday's Child" name her newborn baby?

717) McCoy once claimed "I will not peddle _____. I'm a physician".
    a. roses
    b. flesh
    c. life
    d. bones

718) Edith Keeler in "City On The Edge of Forever", wanted to see a movie starring
    a. Cary Grant
    b. Clark Gable
    c. Buster Keaton
    d. Errol Flynn

719) The planet Vulcan has no moon. True or false?

. . . Answers

712. None

713. Bridge

714. a

715. True

716. Leonard James Akaar

717. b

718. b

719. True

720) How many "throats may be cut in one night by a running man"?

    a. twelve

    b. four thousand

    c. twelve hundred

    d. four hundred

721) Scotty wears a kilt in which TV episode?

    a. "Amok Time"

    b. "Savage Curtain"

    c. "Corbomite Maneuver"

    d. "Wolf In The Fold"

722) Spock once claimed logic was a wreath of "pretty flowers that smell _____."

    a. bad

    b. sweet

    c. rotten

    d. divine

723) Scotty called Ambassador Fox a

    a. popinjay

    b. louse

    c. designer

    d. will o' a wisp

724) What did the Horta use to bore through solid rock?

. . . Answers

720. b

721. b

722. a

723. a

724. Acid

725) Kor claimed he didn't "trust men who _____ much!"
   a. smile
   b. talk
   c. fight
   d. drank

726) What was Kirk and Spock's hourly pay rate in "City On The Edge Of Forever"?

727) In *Star Trek III*, Dr. McCoy's father's name is
   a. Samuel
   b. Leonard
   c. Jacob
   d. David

728) What was Nancy Crater's nickname for Dr. McCoy in "The Man Trap"?

729) Name the race that created the planet in "That Which Survives"?

730) What is the name of the high priestess in "The World Is Hollow And I Have Touched The Sky"?

731) What percentage was the Federation going to get in "Piece of The Action"?

... Answers

725. a

726. 15 cents per hour

727. d

728. Plum

729. Kalandans

730. Natira

731. 40%

732) Kirk gambled his life in "Ultimate Computer" on whose humanity?

    a. Gary Seven
    b. Spock
    c. Commodore Wesley
    d. Commodore Decker

733) Chekov once said vodka was invented by a "little old lady from _____".

734) Khan mentioned whom at the end of "Space Seed"?

    a. Shakespeare
    b. Milton
    c. Grant
    d. Lincoln

735) What class planet is visited in "That Which Survives"?

736) What drink did Balok offer Kirk?

    a. Saurian Brandy
    b. Romulan Ale
    c. Tranya
    d. Tryouvia

737) What did V'ger need to evolve in *Star Trek: The Motion Picture*?

    a. human characteristics
    b. time
    c. infinite knowledge
    d. wisdom

. . . Answers

732. c

733. Leningrad

734. b

735. M

736. c

737. a

738) Cochrane's name for the cloud creature in "Metamorphosis" is _____?

739) Complete this line of dialog, "Mr. Spock, I'm sick of your _____-_____ interference!"

740) Who had captured Captain Pike?
   a. Talosians
   b. Romulans
   c. Klingons
   d. Menninians

741) Mr. Spock tells Captain Kirk that V'ger's home planet is populated by living machines in *Star Trek: The Motion Picture*. True or false?

742) Uhura can speak Swahili. True or false?

743) The USS *Constellation* has no visible serial number. True or false?

744) The planet Argelius was the scene of grisly murders charged to Scottie in what episode?

745) What is the setting for the birth of Eleen's child in "Friday's Child".
   a. a hospital
   b. a mountain cave
   c. The *Enterprise*
   d. None of the above

. . . Answers

738. The companion

739. Half-breed

740. a

741. True

742. True

743. False

744. "Wolf In The Fold"

745. b

QUESTIONS

746) What famous actress is STAR TREK's Ricardo Montalban's sister-in-law?

747) What actress portrayed the Romulan Commander in "Enterprise Incident"?

748) What machine was used to transfer people to the past in "All Our Yesterdays"?

749) NCC-1701/7 is the serial number of what craft?
   a. *Enterprise*
   b. *LaBaron*
   c. *Reliant*
   d. *Galileo*

750) What actor portrayed Ayelbourne in "Errand of Mercy"?

751) Complete this line of dialog. "If we let out a yell, I want an armed party down there before the _____ dies".
   a. planet
   b. sound
   c. echo
   d. monster

752) What was the name of the chief mining engineer in "Devil in The Dark"?

753) Spock stayed behind for awhile in his accelerated level to make repairs in "Wink of An Eye". True or false?

. . . Answers

746. Loretta Young

747. Joanne Linville

748. Atavachron

749. d

750. John Abbott

751. c

752. Vanderberg

753. True

754) What is the name of the Orion woman inmate in "Whom Gods Destroy"?

755) At first, the inhabitants in "The World Is Hollow And I Have Touched The Sky", were aware their planet was not "real". True or false?

756) It had been "four years, seven months and an odd number of days" since Kirk had seen
    a. Areel Shaw
    b. Janice Lester
    c. Edith Keeler
    d. Finnegan

757) What was Kirk and Spock's apartment number in "City On The Edge of Forever"?
    a. 22B
    b. 4B
    c. 12
    d. 21

758) What is the name of the Medusan's female traveling companion in "Is There No Truth In Beauty"?

759) What was the name of the alien commander in "Corbomite Maneuver"?

760) What was Charlie's last name in "Charlie X"?

761) Who was the mystical ruler in "Return Of The Archons"?

. . . *Answers*

754. Marta

755. False (later)

756. a

757. d

758. Dr. Miranda Jones

759. Balok

760. Evans

761. Landru

762) Dr. McCoy once suggested Kirk go on a diet? True or false?

763) William Shatner appeared with Steve McQueen in the TV series FOR THE PEOPLE. True or false?

764) What is the *Enterprise*'s serial number?

765) There were five starships that appeared in "The Ultimate Computer". The *Potemkin*, the *Hook*, the *Lexington*, the *Excaliber* and what other?

766) Complete this line of dialog "Sir, there is a _____ creature crawling on your shoulder".
    a. multilegged
    b. disgusting
    c. Vegulon
    d. none of the above

767) What is the name of the rock creature in "Savage Curtain"?

768) What is Plasus' daughter's name in "Cloudminders"?

769) Complete this line of dialog, "I don't know what's causing it—virus, bacteria or _____, but I'm working on it".
    a. mass hysteria
    b. evil spirits
    c. Rygilian fever
    d. drug overdose

. . . *Answers*

762. True

763. True

764. NCC 1701

765. *Enterprise*

766. a

767. Yarnek

768. Droxine

769. b

770) What was the cause of the pain in Kirk's hands in "Deadly Years"?

771) What actor portrayed Akuta in "The Apple"?

772) The only episode where Mr. Scott uses Captain Kirk's first name is
    a. "Mirror, Mirror"
    b. "Corbomite Maneuver"
    c. "Wolf In The Fold"
    d. "Space Seed"

773) Who portrayed Sybo in "Wolf In The Fold"?

774) Where is Kirk when Decker takes over the *Enterprise* in "Doomsday Machine"?

775) The Horta's life cycle is
    a. 50,000 years
    b. 50 years
    c. 10,000 years
    d. 100 years

776) Over what state was the *Enterprise* spotted and classified as a UFO in "Tomorrow Is Yesterday"?

777) What successful science fiction writer wrote the episode "Shore Leave"?

. . . *Answers*

770. Arthritis

771. Keith Andes

772. a

773. Pilar Seurat

774. *Constellation*

775. a

776. Nebraska

777. Theodore Sturgeon

778) What was the Horta's life form based on?
   a. Carbon
   b. Copper
   c. Silicon
   d. Chrylon

779) At what Starbase does the court-martial take place in "Court-Martial"?

780) The children in "Miri" sickened and died when they reached _____.

781) What actor portrayed the Romulan commander in "Balance of Terror"?

782) The "Red Hour" began at what time?
   a. noon
   b. 6 a.m.
   c. midnight
   d. 6 p.m.

783) Who delivers Eleen's baby in "Friday's Child"?

784) According to Kang, "only a fool fights" where?
   a. in a burning house
   b. in a fiery temple
   c. in an open arena
   d. in a burning starship

785) In "Operation: Annihilate", Spock becomes a guinea pig only after he is infected by the aliens. True or false?

. . . Answers

778. c

779. Starbase 12

780. Puberty

781. Mark Lenard

782. d

783. McCoy

784. a

785. True

786) Kirk physically prevents whom from saving his girlfriend's life in "City On The Edge Of Forever"?

787) A life can be saved by how many drops of Cordrazine?
    a. 6
    b. 10
    c. 2
    d. 12

788) Captain Decker is demoted to a commander and takes on the title of ＿＿＿＿ ＿＿＿＿, in *Star Trek: The Motion Picture*.

789) What happens to Captain Kirk when Elaan cried, in "Elaan of Troyius"?

790) Who are the Kohm's enemies in "Omega Glory"?

791) Spock's consciousness was hidden in whose body in "Return To Tomorrow"?

792) What actor portrayed Oxmyx in "Piece of The Action"?

793) How many years will it take Cyrano Jones to clear the space station of tribbles?
    a. 20.7
    b. 18.6
    c. 12.7
    d. 17.9

. . . Answers

786. McCoy

787. c

788. Executive Officer

789. He falls in love with her

790. Yangs

791. Nurse Chapel

792. Anthony Caruso

793. d

794) Through what shaft does the creature enter a crewman's cabin in "Obsession"?

795) What actor portrayed Tyree in "Private Little War"?

796) Thelev is a member of what party in "Journey To Babel"?

797) Dr. McCoy explains that Tribbles must "be born _____".

798) *Kaladonia* is the name of the starship larger than the starship *Enterprise*. True or false?

799) The *Intrepid* was the name of the destroyed starship in "The Immunity Syndrome". What kind of vessel was it?
   a. Triskelion
   b. Andorian
   c. Vulcan
   d. None of the above

800) This STAR TREK actor starred in the TV series, FANTASY ISLAND.

801) The sound effect later used for the tricorder sound is used in "Return Of The Archons" to accompany the materializing of what character?

. . . *Answers*

794. Ventilation shaft

795. Michael Witney

796. Andorian

797. Pregnant

798. False

799. c

800. Ricardo Montalban

801. Landru

802) In *Star Trek: The Motion Picture*, V'ger is really
_____.
   a. Voyager 4
   b. Voyager 6
   c. all of the above
   d. none of the above

803) Gary Seven's apartment number in "Assignment:
Earth" was
   a. 12B
   b. 22B
   c. 3A
   d. 12A

804) The creature steals an important part of what re-
actor in "Devil in the Dark".
   a. PXK
   b. Boiler
   c. PBB
   d. none of the above

805) What is the chess move Scotty asks Kirk to respond to in "Whom Gods Destroy"?

806) What was the name of the mission in "City On
The Edge of Forever"?
   a. 48th Street Mission
   b. 42nd Street Mission
   c. 21st Street Mission
   d. none of the above

. . . Answers

802. b

803. a

804. a

805. Queen to Queen's level 3

806. c

807) What is the name of the governing computer in "The World Is Hollow And I Have Touched The Sky"?

808) Marvick is one of the men who designed what on the *Enterprise* in "Is There No Truth In Beauty"?

809) Law of Parallel Planet Development.
    a. Murphy's
    b. Hodgkins
    c. Sargon's
    d. Corrigan's

810) Name the cargo ship that brought Charlie to the *Enterprise* in "Charlie X".

811) In *Star Trek: The Motion Picture*, Commander Decker and Lieutenant Ilia meet, for the first time, on the *Enterprise*. True or false?

812) What was the title of the second pilot for the STAR TREK series?
    a. "The Cage"
    b. "The Corbomite Maneuver"
    c. "Day of The Dove"
    d. "Where No Man Has Gone Before"

813) What was the name of the alien's ship in "Corbomite Maneuver"?

. . . Answers

807. The Oracle

808. Engines

809. b

810. *Antares*

811. False

812. d

813. *Fesarius*

814) General Order Seven is
    a. Death Penalty
    b. Destruct Order
    c. Evacuation Order
    d. Incarceration Penalty

815) The "salt" creature's true appearance was revealed when it died in "The Man Trap". True or false?

816) William Shatner had not worked with actress France Nuyon prior to STAR TREK. True or false?

817) In "Trouble With Tribbles", what did Kirk order from the food processors?

818) Complete Khan's line of dialog in Star Trek II, "Let them eat _____".
    a. cake
    b. static
    c. dust
    d. none of the above

819) On what planet is a huge library discovered in "All Our Yesterdays"?

820) What is the name of Ardan's High Advisor in "Cloudminders"?

821) Name the make-up artist responsible for the aging appearances in "Deadly Years".

. . . *Answers*

814. a

815. True

816. False (Broadway)

817. Chicken sandwich and coffee

818. b

819. Sarpeidon

820. Plasus

821. Fred Phillips

822) The actor who portrayed Makora in "Apple" also portrayed Ken Hutchinson in what TV series?

823) In "What Are Little Girls Made of", android Kirk claimed Kirk's brother had how many sons?
    a. one
    b. six
    c. three
    d. two

824) The music heard while Kara dances in "Wolf in the Fold" was also heard in the dance sequence of what original episode?

825) Decker steals what in an attempt to destroy the planet killer?

826) Captain Christopher's jet was saved by the *Enterprise* tractor beam in "Tomorrow is Yesterday". True or false?

827) Name the character who traps the *Enterprise* and crew in "Squire of Gothos".

828) What is the name of the commodore who institutes the court-martial against Kirk in "Court-Martial"?

829) What actor portrayed Jahn in "Miri"?

830) Mr. Spock speaks the first words of dialog in *Star Trek III*. True or false?

. . . Answers

822. *Starsky and Hutch*

823. c

824. "The Cage"

825. Shuttlecraft

826. False

827. Trelane

828. L.T. Stone

829. Michael J. Pollard

830. False (Kirk speaks first)

831) Who is responsible for the death of the current Teer in "Friday's Child"?

832) At what age did Cochrane decide he wanted to die in space?

833) The aliens in "Operation: Annihilate" affect what system in the human body?

834) "Precisely" how far from the door did Miranda Jones claim to be in "Is There No Truth In Beauty"?
   a. One meter, four centimeters
   b. One meter, one centimeter
   c. One meter, twelve centimeters
   d. Twelve meters, four centimeters

835) What is Kirk's final line in "City On The Edge of Forever"?

836) In "Elaan of Troyius", what is Elaan's necklace made of?

837) The "worship words" used in "Omega Glory" are a distorted version of what?

838) Who uses telepathy to force Nurse Chapel into poisoning Sargon?

839) What actor portrayed Krako in "Piece of the Action"?

. . . *Answers*

831. The Klingons (Kras)

832. 87

833. Nervous

834. a

835. "Let's get the hell out of here."

836. Dilithium Crystals

837. Preamble to the US Constitution

838. Henoch

839. Vic Taybeck

840) Ore ships call at Delta Vega every
   a. 25 years
   b. 30 years
   c. 20 years
   d. 10 years

841) What actor portrayed Ensign Garrovick in "Obsession"?

842) In "Private Little War", the Migato was a deadly insect. True or false?

843) The vessel following the *Enterprise* is discovered to be an _____ vessel?

844) Scotty has a passion for studying what, instead of taking shore leave in "Trouble With Tribbles"?

845) Loki was a character black on the left and white on the right in what episode?
   a. "City On The Edge Of Forever"
   b. "Let This Be Your Last Battlefield"
   c. "The Cage"
   d. none of the above

846) What actress portrayed Shahna in "Gamesters of Triskelion"?

847) What was Ricardo Montalban's character name in FANTASY ISLAND?

. . . *Answers*

840. c

841. Stephen Brooks

842. False (beast)

843. Orion

844. Technical journals

845. b

846. Angelique Pettyjohn

847. Mr. Roarke

848) In the episode "Taste of Armageddon", what planet does the *Enterprise* visit?

849) What actor portrayed Kor in "Errand of Mercy"?

850) Complete this line of dialog "I used a hand phaser and Zap!-_____".
    a. boiling water
    b. chicken soup
    c. hot coffee
    d. they fell

851) The vital part stolen by the creature in "Devil in The Dark" controlled what for the colony?

852) Garth has the ability to change his appearance but not his voice in "Whom Gods Destroy". True or false?

853) What sort of computer projection is the woman in "That Which Survives"?

854) The SS *Botany Bay* originally held how many life support cannisters?
    a. 84
    b. 64
    c. 82
    d. 24

855) What character was Jones' aide in "Is There No Truth In Beauty"?

. . . *Answers*

848. Eminiar 7

849. John Colicos

850. c

851. Life Support

852. False

853. Holographic

854. a

855. Larry Marvick

856) What two members of the underground save Kirk and Spock from being "absorbed" in "Return of The Archons"?

857) The *Galileo* was what kind of vessel?
    a. Starship
    b. Shuttlecraft
    c. Warship
    d. Cruiser

858) What actor portrayed Charlie in "Charlie X"?

859) Complete this line of dialog: "Take D'Artagnan here to _____ _____".
    a. the bridge
    b. the brig
    c. sick bay
    d. his room

860) What was Uhura's only spoken line in "Corbomite Maneuver"?
    a. "Yes, Captain".
    b. "Hailing frequencies opened, sir".
    c. "Enterprise, to Starfleet Command".
    d. none of the above

861) Leonard Nimoy is not listed in the opening acting credits for *Star Trek III*. True or false?

862) Had Saavik ever piloted a starship out of space-dock prior to Kirk's inspection in *Star Trek II*?

. . . Answers

856. Reger and Marplon

857. c

858. Robert Walker, Jr.

859. c

860. b

861. True

862. No

363) What STAR TREK actor originally portrayed the lead in the TV series T. J. HOOKER?

364) What was the date of the newspaper story "FDR Confers with Slum-area 'Angel' "?
   a. Feb. 20, 1936
   b. Feb. 14, 1931
   c. Feb. 23, 1936
   d. Feb. 29, 1934

365) "Revenge is a dish that is best served cold" is whose proverb?

366) What is the name of the aged librarian in "All Our Yesterdays"?

367) Complete this line of Spock's dialog "The parabolic intersection of dimension with _____".

368) In "City On The Edge of Forever", Kirk bought what for himself to eat?
   a. chicken sandwich and coffee
   b. ham on rye
   c. bologna and a hard roll
   d. a roll and coffee

369) What character was called a "chair bound paper pusher" in "Deadly Years"?

370) What actor portrayed Makora in "The Apple"?

. . . *Answers*

863. William Shatner

864. c

865. Klingon

866. Mr. Atoz (A-to-Z)

867. Dimension

868. c

869. Commodore Stocker

870. David Soul

871) The destruction of what system leads the *Enterprise* to discover a unique power source in "The Changeling"?

872) What malfunction almost prevents Kirk from escaping the *Constellation* in "Doomsday"?

873) A polaroid camera was used by Captain Christopher to photograph the *Enterprise* in flight in "Tomorrow Is Yesterday". True or false?

874) Who is finally able to rescue Kirk and the *Enterprise* from their capture in "Squire of Gothos"?

875) Complete this line of dialog, "That was the equation! Existence. Survival must cancel out _____".
    a. programming
    b. existence
    c. life
    d. explanation

876) What was the name of the eccentric lawyer Kirk retains to defend him in "Court-Martial"?

877) What character did the children first abduct in "Miri"?

878) Who is the only performer in STAR TREK to have portrayed a Vulcan, a Romulan, and a Klingon?

. . . *Answers*

871. Maluriam

872. Transporter

873. False

874. Trelane's parents

875. a

876. Samuel Cogley

877. Yeoman Rand

878. Mark Lenard

879) Kirk communicates with the cloud creature with a universal _____.

880) What actor portrayed Peter in "Operation: Annihilate"?

881) What award did "City On The Edge Of Forever" win for the STAR TREK series in 1968?

882) Spock is accused of being a relative of what dark figure in "Omega Glory"?

883) What actress portrayed Dr. Mulhall in "Return to Tomorrow"?

884) What STAR TREK actor also starred as Mel in the TV series ALICE?

885) Dr. McCoy faced a similar test as Garrovick years earlier in "Obsession". True or false?

886) Captain Kirk and crew are abducted to what planet in "Gamesters of Triskelion"?

887) Thelev is actually an altered _____, pretending to be a Tellerite.

. . . Answers

879. Translator

880. Craig Hundley

881. International Hugo Award for Science Fiction

882. Satan

883. Diana Muldaur

884. Vic Taybeck

885. False (Kirk)

886. Triskelion

887. Orion

QUESTIONS

888) "Mr. Sulu, if I'd wanted a Russian history lesson, I'd have brought _____".
    a. Mr. Chekov
    b. Mr. Spock
    c. Dr. McCoy
    d. Ensign Pulver

889) What actor portrayed Jones in "Trouble With Tribbles"?

890) In "City On The Edge Of Forever", McCoy goes mad when he accidentally injected himself with Cordrazine. True or false?

891) The triad was the name given to the Arena in "The Gamester of Triskelion". True or false?

892) What actress portrayed Marla McGivers in "Space Seed"?

893) What was the character name of the council head in "Taste of Armageddon"?

894) John Colicos of "Errand of Mercy" also appeared as what character in "Battlestar Galactica"?

895) Spock asks Kirk to do what with the creature before it would be destroyed?

. . . Answers

888. a

889. Stanley Adams

890. True

891. True

892. Madlyn Rhue

893. Anon 7

894. Baltar

895. Communicate

QUESTIONS

896) In "City On The Edge Of Forever", what newspaper carried the heading "FDR Confers With Slum-area 'Angel' "?

    a. *New York Times*
    b. *Star-Dispatch*
    c. *Daily Star*
    d. *Free Press*

897) At the opening of "City On The Edge Of Forever", who was Dr. McCoy's patient on the bridge?

898) What civilization originally built Yonada in "World Is Hollow And I Have Touched The Sky"?

899) The sight of the Medusa without a protective visor can cause what?

900) The mystical ruler in "Return of the Archons" was really a _____.

901) Charlie was the lone survivor of a crash on what planet?

902) What actor portrayed the alien commander in "The Corbomite Maneuver"?

903) What was Kirk's reply to Scotty's chess problem code in "Whom Gods Destroy"?

    a. Queen to King's Level 3
    b. King to King's Level One
    c. Queen to King's Level One
    d. None of the above

. . . Answers

896. b

897. Mr. Sulu

898. Fabrini

899. Insanity

900. Computer

901. Thasus

902. Clint Howard

903. c

904) What is Kirk's rank in *Star Trek II*?

905) James Doohan was a skilled airplane mechanic prior to STAR TREK, in the Royal Canadian Air Force. True or false?

906) *Reliant*'s command console would respond to what type of code from the *Enterprise* in *Star Trek II*?

907) Spock discussed his mating cycle with Droxine in "Cloudminders". True or false?

908) What actor portrayed Stocker in "Deadly Years"?

909) The trouble in "Mirror, Mirror" begins after diplomatic relations have been started with what council?

910) The space probe with enormous power in "The Changeling" was called _____?

911) What ship's engines are exploded to destroy the planet killer?

912) Spock must return to Vulcan during Pon Far, or what will happen to him in "Amok Time"?

913) What STAR TREK actor provided the voice of Trelane's father in "Squire of Gothos"?

914) What did Dr. McCoy use to single out Finnegan's heartbeat in "Court-Martial"?

. . . Answers

904. Admiral

905. False

906. Prefix

907. True

908. Charles Drake

909. Halkan

910. Nomad

911. *Constellation*

912. Die

913. James Doohan

914. White Sound Device

915) What did Anton Karidian do for a living?

916) Widen was the brand name on the milk truck in what episode?
    a. "Dagger of the Mind"
    b. "Who Mourns For Adonais"
    c. "The Menagerie"
    d. "The City On The Edge Of Forever"

917) Mark Lenard made his first appearance in STAR TREK in "Balance of Terror". True or false?

918) What actress portrayed Elaan of Troyius?

919) The cloud creature unites with what character to save her life, in "Metamorphosis"?

920) The actor who portrayed Peter in "Operation: Annihilate" also appeared in what episode?

921) What famous science fiction writer wrote "City On The Edge Of Forever"?

922) What are the two counterparts of the Kohms and Yangs discovered by Kirk in "Omega Glory"?

923) What sector of Genesis is Mr. Spock's "body" found in, in *Star Trek III?*
    a. Sector 2
    b. Sector 3
    c. Sector 4
    d. Sector 8

. . . *Answers*

915. Actor

916. d

917. True

918. France Nuyen

919. Nancy Hedford

920. "And The Children Shall Lead"

921. Harlan Ellison

922. Communists, Yankees

923. b

924) What planet does the *Enterprise* visit in "Patterns Of Force"?

925) The only time Kirk is shown using a surface vehicle is in what episode?

926) If Garrovick hadn't delayed firing in "Obsession", the gaseous creature would have been destroyed. True or false?

927) In what "trinary" star system is Triskelion?

928) What was the real name of Spock's favorite "pet" as a child?

929) What actor portrayed Captain Koloth in "Trouble With Tribbles"?

930) Sylvia turns into what, crushing the other alien in "Cat's Paw"?

931) What DYNASTY TV series star once appeared in a STAR TREK episode?

932) What is Kirk's Indian name in "Paradise Syndrome"?

933) What STAR TREK actress appeared in *Tootsie* and *Mr. Mom*?

. . . *Answers*

924. Ekos

925. "Piece of The Action"

926. False

927. M-24 Alpha

928. Sehlet

929. William Campbell

930. Giant black cat

931. Joan Collins

932. Medicine Chief Kirok

933. Teri Garr

934) Complete Kirk's line of dialog to Spock in "Patterns of Force". "I don't care if you hit the broadside of a _____, Mr. Spock."

935) Complete this line of dialog by Mr. Scott when describing one final bottle of liquor in "By Any Other Name". "It's _____!"

936) Both Mr. Chekov and Mr. Spock volunteer for the mission in "Immunity Syndrome". True or false?

937) Kirk had visited the planet in "Private Little War" how many years earlier?

938) What actor portrayed Septimus in "Bread and Circuses"?

939) What was the character name of Barris's assistant in "Trouble With Tribbles"?

940) "Kroykah" is the word for immediate "stop" in what language?
   a. Ardanian
   b. English
   c. Vulcan
   d. Klingon

941) Zephram Cochrane was born on Earth. True or false?

942) What was the character name of the woman Spock was attracted to in "This Side of Paradise"?

. . . _Answers_

934. Barn

935. Green

936. False

937. Thirteen

938. Ian Wolfe

939. Arne Darvin

940. c

941. False

942. Leila Kalomi

QUESTIONS

943) What actor portrayed Ambassador Fox in "Taste of Armageddon"?

944) The character of Mr. Leslie was seen in only one episode during the series. True or false?

945) The costume expert who worked the Horta in "Devil In The Dark", also played the "Dancing Bear" on the ANDY WILLIAMS SHOW. True or false?

946) What is the name given the woman who attacks the *Enterprise* crew in "That Which Survives"?

947) What is the name of the planet leader in "Plato's Stepchildren"?

948) Gem cannot speak in "Empath". True or false?

949) Kirk is forced to list Commander Decker and Lieutenant Ilia as casualties in his report to Starfleet after the mission is completed in *Star Trek: The Motion Picture*. True or false?

950) The actor who portrayed Gorgan in "And The Children Shall Lead" is also a noted _____. •

951) What did the Air Force security man order to eat on board the *Enterprise* in "Tomorrow is Yesterday"?

952) A transporter malfunction divides Mr. Spock into two people in the "Enemy Within". True or false?

. . . *Answers*

943. Gene Lyons

944. False

945. True

946. Losira

947. Parmen

948. True

949. False

950. Attorney

951. Chicken Soup

952. False (Capt Kirk)

953) On what hand does Khan wear a glove in *Star Trek II*?

954) What actor was originally cast as "Bones" McCoy?

955) Who was born on August 19, 1921 in El Paso, Texas?

956) What actor portrayed Admiral Kirk in *Star Trek II*?

957) What does Spock use on Lester to get to the truth of the matter in "Turnabout Intruder"?

958) What planet does the *Enterprise* visit in "Requiem For Methuselah"?

959) Who does Kirk and crew discover is a guest of the Androids in "I, Mudd"?

960) What member of the landing party is not affected by the strange disease in "Deadly Years"?

961) Nomad believes it must now destroy what kind of life forms?

962) Kirk and McCoy take Scotty to what plane in "Wolf In the Fold"?

. . . Answers

953. Right

954. DeForest Kelly

955. Gene Roddenberry

956. William Shatner

957. Vulcan mind meld

958. Holberg 917-6

959. Harry Mudd

960. Chekov

961. Imperfect

962. Argelius Two

963) The actress who portrayed T'Pau was married to what famous actor:

    a. Peter Lorre
    b. Cary Grant
    c. Humphrey Bogart
    d. none of the above

964) Name the alien Kirk encountered in "Alternate Factor".

965) Name the only two part episode in STAR TREK.

966) In Admiral Kirk's absence, Genesis had become a galactic controversy in *Star Trek III*. True or false?

967) "Conscience of The King" was the last appearance of Lt. Kevin Riley. True or false?

968) The director of "Tantalus Five" was what character?

969) In "Who Mourns Adonais", the god wishes the crew to stay on what planet?

970) What actress portrayed Nancy Hedford in "Metamorphosis"?

971) What device did the aliens in "Cat's Paw" use to assume human form?

972) In what episode did a DYNASTY star once appear?

. . . Answers

963. a

964. Lazarus

965. "The Menagerie"

966. True

967. True

968. Dr. Tristan Adams

969. Pollux IV

970. Elinor Donahue

971. Transmuter

972. "City On The Edge Of Forever"

973) What actress portrayed Miramanee in "Paradise Syndrome"?

974) What was the name given the computer console in "Assignment: Earth"?

975) What actor portrayed John Gill in "Patterns of Force"?

976) Name the alien in "By Any Other Name" that Scotty set about getting drunk?

977) What Federation vessel visited the planet in "Piece of the Action" prior to the *Enterprise*?

978) In "Obsession", it is said that Kirk served as a lieutenant on what ship?

979) Who is trying to take over the planet in "Private Little War"?

980) What was the name of the Klingon Commander in "Trouble With Tribbles"?

981) Do starships ever land on planet surfaces in the STAR TREK series?

982) The *Enterprise* bridge in *Star Trek III*, was located on what sound stage at Paramount Pictures during production.
    a. Stage 5   c. Stage 9
    b. Stage 8   d. Stage 15

. . . Answers

973. Sabrina Scharf

974. Beta Five

975. David Brian

976. Tomar

977. USS *Horizon*

978. USS *Farragut*

979. Klingons

980. Captain Koloth

981. No

982. c

983) There were two episodes that mentioned cor-bomite: "The Corbomite Maneuver" and
   a. "The Deadly Years"
   b. "Dagger of the Mind"
   c. "City On the Edge of Forever"
   d. "Obsession"

984) Spock's "girlfriend" in "This Side Of Paradise" was of what profession?

985) The *Enterprise* pulls up along a late 20th Century _____ _____ in "Space Seed"?

986) Mr. Leslie delivers no dialog in "This Side of Paradise". True or false?

987) Complete Dr. McCoy's line in "Devil in the Dark". "I'm a doctor, not a _____".

988) Dr. McCoy injects himself with an overdose of what drug in "City On The Edge Of Forever"?

989) The *Enterprise* intercepts a stolen Federation _____ in "Let This Be Your Last Battlefield".

990) What is the name of the dwarf jester in "Plato's Stepchildren"?

991) The Empath has the ability to absorb injuries and pain into her own body. True or false?

. . . Answers

983. a

984. Botanist

985. Sleeper ship

986. False

987. Bricklayer

988. Cordrazine

989. Shuttlecraft

990. Alexander

991. True

992) What child actress portrayed Mary Janowski in "And The Children Shall Lead"?

993) Who served the transported security guard in "Tomorrow Is Yesterday" something to eat?

994) Who led the stranded landing party in "The Enemy Within"?

995) What actor portrayed Khan in *Star Trek II*?

996) DeForest Kelly appeared with Richard Widmark as a villain in the movie *Warlock*. True or false?

997) Gene Roddenberry co-wrote the book *The Making Of Star Trek*. True or false?

998) As mentioned in *Star Trek III*, how many times had Kirk taken the Kobayaski Maru test?

999) Mr. Spock is rendered unconscious after his mind meld with V'ger in *Star Trek: The Motion Picture*. True or false?

1000) The *Enterprise* landing party beam down to whose residence in "Requiem For Methuselah"?

1001) Mudd proclaims himself to be what of the android planet in "I, Mudd"?

1002) On what TV network was STAR TREK originally seen?

. . . Answers

992. Pamelyn Ferdin

993. Transporter Chief Kyle

994. Sulu

995. Ricardo Montalban

996. True

997. True

998. Three

999. True

1000. Mr. Flint

1001. Emperor

1002. NBC

QUESTIONS

1003) What "unit" does Nomad offer to restore in "The Changeling"?

1004) Scotty had suffered an accidental head injury in "Wolf in the Fold". True or false?

1005) What character "gets the girl" at the end of "Amok Time"?

1006) What did Lazarus steal, crucial to the *Enterprise* in "Alternate Factor"?

1007) Captain Pike had not visited Talos IV before Spock abducted him in "The Menagerie". True or false?

1008) From what Shakespearean play did Karidian quote when confronted by Lieutenant Riley?

1009) The inmate who escaped to the *Enterprise* was identified as Adam's assistant, Dr. _____.

1010) What does Apollo want the *Enterprise* crew to do in "Who Mourns Adonais"?

1011) What STAR TREK actress played a regular in the series FATHER KNOWS BEST?

1012) What happens to the aliens after they turn into fragile creatures in the end of "Cat's Paw"?

. . . *Answers*

1003. Mr. Scott

1004. True

1005. Stonn

1006. Dilithium Crystals

1007. False

1008. *Hamlet*

1009. Simon Van Gelder

1010. Worship him

1011. Elinor Donahue

1012. Die

1013) Joan Collins appeared in MISSION IMPOSSIBLE as Jim Phelps' love interest. True or false?

1014) Who wrote "Enterprise Incident"?

1015) Lee Cronin is the pen name of what STAR TREK writer?

1016) Who is M-5's "creator" in "Ultimate Computer"?

1017) Name the alien Kirk sets out to seduce in "By Any Other Name"?

1018) How long had it been since the first Federation vessel had visited the planet in "Piece of The Action"?

1019) Under what commander did Kirk serve on the USS *Farragut*?

1020) What segment of the population do the Klingons arm in "Private Little War"?

1021) Babel is the code name for a planet in "Journey to Babel". True or false?

1022) What was the name of the "space trader" in "Trouble With Tribbles"?

1023) What is the name of the "old flame" Kirk meets again in "Shore Leave"?

. . . Answers

1013. True

1014. D.C. Fontana

1015. Gene L. Coon

1016. Dr. Richard Daystrom

1017. Kelinda

1018. 100 years

1019. Captain Garrovick

1020. Hill people

1021. True

1022. Cyrano Jones

1023. Ruth

1024) Spock and Sarek are not "on speaking terms" when they first encounter each other in "Journey To Babel". True or false?

1025) Kirk once wished for "a beach to walk on . . . a few days, no braid on my shoulder". True or false?

... *Answers*

1024. True

1025. True

FAVORITE GROSS SELECTIONS
by Julius Alvin

GROSS JOKES (1244, $2.50)
You haven't read it all—until you read GROSS JOKES! This complete compilation is guaranteed to deliver the sickest, sassiest laughs!

TOTALLY GROSS JOKES (1333, $2.50)
From the tasteless ridiculous to the taboo sublime, TOTALLY GROSS JOKES has enough laughs in store for even *the most* particular humor fanatics.

UTTERLY GROSS JOKES (1350, $2.50)
The best of tasteless, tacky, revolting, insulting, appalling, foul, lewd, and mortifying jokes—jokes so sick they're UTTERLY GROSS!

EXTREMELY GROSS JOKES (1600, $2.50)
Beyond the humor of gross, totally gross, and utterly gross jokes there is only the laughter of EXTREMELY GROSS JOKES!

GROSS LIMERICKS (1375, $2.50)
This masterpiece collection offers the funniest of rhythmical rhymes, from all your favorite categories of humor. And they're true-to-form, honest-to-goodness, GROSS LIMERICKS!

GROSS LIMERICKS VOLUME II (1616, $2.50)
Rhyming limericks so bold, sassy, and savvy they'll leave you laughing right through the night with delight!

GROSS GIFTS (1111, $2.50)
It's the Encyclopedia Grossitanica, with everything from gross books to gross cosmetics, and from gross movies to gross vacations. It's all here in the thoroughly and completely tasteless and tacky catalogue we call . . . GROSS GIFTS!

Available wherever paperbacks are sold, or order direct from the Publisher. Send cover price plus 50¢ per copy for mailing and handling to Zebra Books, Dept. 1732, 475 Park Avenue South, New York, N.Y. 10016. DO NOT SEND CASH.

CAPTIVATING ROMANCE FROM ZEBRA